JACKLEG OPERA

Jackleg Opera
Collected Poems, 1990 to 2013

BJ Ward

North Atlantic Books
Berkeley, CA

Published by
North Atlantic Books
Berkeley, California

Cover photo © iStockphoto.com/Steven Hayes
Cover and book design by Jasmine Hromjak
Printed in the United States of America

Jackleg Opera: Collected Poems, 1990 to 2013 is sponsored and published by the Society for the Study of Native Arts and Sciences (dba North Atlantic Books), an educational nonprofit based in Berkeley, California, that collaborates with partners to develop cross-cultural perspectives, nurture holistic views of art, science, the humanities, and healing, and seed personal and global transformation by publishing work on the relationship of body, spirit, and nature.

North Atlantic Books' publications are available through most bookstores. For further information, visit our website at www.northatlanticbooks.com or call 800-733-3000.

Library of Congress Cataloging-in-Publication Data

Ward, BJ.
    [Poems. Selections]
    Jackleg Opera: collected poems, 1990 to 2013 / BJ Ward.
        pages cm. — (Io Poetry Series)
    ISBN 978-1-58394-677-0
    I. Title.
    PS3623.A7314J33 2013

    811'.— dc23

                                              2013008257

2 3 4 5 6 7 8 OPM 20 19 18 17 16

North Atlantic Books is committed to the protection of our environment. We partner with FSC-certified printers using soy-based inks and print on recycled paper whenever possible.

For My Brother,
Michael Ward

Contents

Gravedigger's Birthday (2002)   67

Jackleg Opera: New Poems (2013)

(T)he city is built
To music, therefore never built at all,
And therefore built for ever.

—Alfred, Lord Tennyson

Man, there's an opera out on the Turnpike....

—Bruce Springsteen

17 Becomes 43

My dear, / How could you have let this happen to you?

—Hayden Carruth ("Memory," *Dr. Jazz*)

Whatever happened to Hills Diner?
What became of the sugar
shaker we'd pass around the booth,
a baton our tongues were racing with?
Or the blunt table jukebox,
a torah that offered answers
a quarter a pop?
My fingers flipped the pages
till I found the evening's sermon.
Where did the others go?
I was the sorry ship designed to do nothing
but imagine, soldered with wonder,
floating toward these icebergs.
Did anyone else survive? Who disassembled the coffee?
Was it put together again?
O Karen Carswell, with your foreign brassiere,
thou queen of patience! Where have you been?
Does the sky, with its unfolding dream, remain
what you hold dear?
Are you still on a peak in Darien?
And our waitress—the beautiful, undiluted waitress—
what can she bring us now
and is her beehive still towering?

A Late Memoriam for Tommy Whuzizname, Because Nobody Ever Talks about That Prick Anymore

30 years dead now—buried in the cornfield, near the scrub oak—
a bitter boy growing into sweet corn: grotesque
and illegal, sure, but his folks, all dead now too, were too broke
for any formal plot.
               In high school he'd sit with head on desk
always in the corner farthest from the teacher—
hair grown wild, mangled glasses on his cloyed face—
a face I saw thrill just a week before he'd disappear,
howling at the quarry, drinking shit beer and his father's Chivas
with us other jerks, smoking Marlboros from a hard box
in the woods' dark. He would smile then, a plowed row of ignored teeth
that shined when the whiskey's rain softened his chin and cheeks—
his laugh bloomed huge at the edge of the campfire's bearable girth.
In class he would keep his hands at his side, but there
under the stars and long-necked pines his arms would flail,
animating plots, pick-up lines, and ill-conceived dares,
all indicia of a latent sour-ass charm no school could curtail.
When the cops came our clutch scattered into mini-nations,
through back yards, under clothes lines. Their comminations
were a hot breeze inspiring Tommy and me into the cornfield. The trees
smelled of smoldering and the ground was starting to freeze.

We laughed and hooted and stuck our fingers out all the way across,
like masts on pirate ships:

                        our bodies scudding from man-made laws.
All that lobo know-how made our Chucky Ts rubber paws,
and stalks of corn moved with the kerf our escaping caused.
We didn't know it then: we were running both from and to hell—
past the scrub oak, across the ground that would be Tommy's final jail cell—
from the black and white, through sweetness. No portfolios or hair gel.
We learned lessons as we ran, alive and doing quite well.

Upon Reading Plato's *Allegory of the Cave* on a Smart Phone

The dawn's birds sing truth as I rise
and footsteps are sincere. What then though?
At every exit the highway aims French fries
at all the fat kids thumbing Nintendo.

The news broadcasts obfuscation
the way a shotgun broadcasts buckshot—
delivered by the pretty people who overtook the station.
(The rest of us are peripatetic mugshots.)

A nation observes the 4:00 stock closing
as if it were its temple bell dinging—
Turn off this noise. It is engrossing
the birdsong, the footsteps, the stars hissing & singing.

My friends are so thirsty with water in their eyes
so back to the well we'll crawl:
Tell Plato to rise and re-philosophize—
Facebook is the new cave wall—

Baseball 1980

Hostages in Iran
    but the only globe
I concerned myself with

was the Rawlings
    dormant fastball
I gripped like Bruce Sutter,

squeezing it
    as if to expel its juice—
as if to press hits out of it.

The field smelled of immensity.
    Air Force planes practiced
maneuvers over power lines

as I fingered the 216 stitches
    like a Morse code that was all
dashes. It said I might suffer.

It said I was twelve
    and the world was old.
I palmed the encrypted globe

into circulation.
    I stood on the mound—
not as a sovereign

but rather like an appellate
    beseeching dead pitchers
to make me hide

what I'd not show—
    to guide my round dart
woodlessly to mitt.

At twelve, speed and blur were all.
    How could I know then
there was no need

to make that world go more quickly?
    If I learned to deceive artfully,
I could create a new truth.

My mother would soon call for me
    to eat, and the evening news would sweep
from far away into our living room.

But the batter was in the box.
    The catcher's glove half-opened
like a semi-colon.

I knew so little of what I was doing—

perhaps the answers were there
in the language: Strike. Foul. Watch

for the attempted steal.
    I argued with the signs
and tried to make sorrow

out of what we played with.
    I chewed gum.
The flavor didn't last long.

The ruminating did.

Building Codes

"dear BJ, why is new jersey so strong in poets and corrupt politicians?
Is there some connection?"

Dear Tony,

While New York has the Macy's Day Parade,
Jersey has 44 politicians perp walking,
makeshift cowls on their heads, slap-
    dashed out of held-up
sweatshirts and newspapers (which
will contain this very moment tomorrow)
to conceal   their faces from
the cameras poised like slingshots,
    hands chained together
        as if we could force prayer
or any other poetry.
                From a distance,
they look like a row of ill-fitted monks
doing their slow, itchy march toward salvation.

When Yeats said, "if it does not seem a moment's thought,
Our stitching and unstitching has been naught,"
        our politicians picked up on it
and that's clear in the courtrooms
        when the guilty seem surprised
by their own actions—
    "Wha—me? I'm not guilty …"
(no surprise in the politician,
      no surprise in the fleeced)

But I almost digressed, Tony—

I am thinking of poets who haven't written
                well in years
but who rubbed against the sun
                twenty years ago—

Aren't they in their own kinds of prisons too?
They hate to think of themselves as arrested
                but there they sit,
unable to move anywhere in their writing
                as people study their old work,
try to learn from it, ask
                in various versions,
                        how did you pull it off?

The old poets answer as obliquely as possible,
                the confessing already done.
In the anthologies, their poems rise like thin buildings
                arranged by secret covenants,
                        with concealed escape routes,
        the construction corporation of Soul & Duende
                        accepting payoffs not realized till the work was done—

a shadow skirrs a receptive palm
        and arenas rise from swamplands.

I think of the rumors here—the bodies like rebars
   in the cement below Giants Stadium
where—   when
       men aren't taking
          each other down—
   people sing snippets
      of classic rock
             anthems
over the sibilant, unseen traffic
   flying out of Newark
and dance between possessions
       in the polluted, deceptive night—
   an unclean atmosphere
      that meets all state regulations.

Studies in Shakespeare

Shakespeare's felicity is so often taught
it is easy to overlook how taut
the sinews in his neck must
have been when he grasped his pen, or the musk
that exuded from the fat of his chin
below a somewhat chthonic grin—
life wrestled death on his desk when he composed.

In class, easier to imagine him reposed:
checking out clouds, musing aloud,
his thoughts an orderly march (not a teeming crowd),
collar Elizabethan-high, deftly and measuredly
elucidating his prosody,
but that's all wrong—

Shakespeare's head revved with song—
a piston at his desk, sitting and standing—
any flourish could send a kingdom failing.
Wild Compassion bedded Insatiable Wonder
and birthed a wisdom that cleaved monarchs asunder.
A combustion of language stoked in his body—a rage
that dictated how he blazed on each page.
The delight of inventing Yorick: gripping
his own skullcap with his left hand, and dipping
the plume in ink with his right—
as if dipping his ken into a pool of deep night,
emerging from that darkness, dripping with news to write—
the joy, the horror, the third-eye sight
(his soul's little flashlight) when he realized

Iago was part of him, the despised
side that Anne Hathaway hated, blamed on his buddies,
but Billy knew from his studies
it was human nature
that weighs down our stature
if found out by the neighbors. The deft
plumbing of himself before he left
work each day—the labors of a man trying
not to be deluded, vying
for even his pockmarks to be included
in his plays. And the rapture of this capture—
O Sweet Venery—in class let it be tuted:
the musk that exuded, his skull's hair—
how each follicle must have fluted foursquare—
and how, after his guts were all confessed,
he just exited his desk
to a patient wife who loved his flair,
perhaps flashing her funky Renaissance sleepwear
as he hustled from his chair to her there,
secretly pursued by bear.

Disgusted with the Endless War, I Turn Off the Evening News and Make Love to My Wife Instead

I pledge allegiance
to how we flag
in our united state
after we make love.

We're on the sheets,
having reaped hugs, licks,
all this bed could stand—

The army has exited
this country, leaving
only the painters
to keep close watch.

My body's politicians
are on a good will junket
to her body's vacation spot,
and her body's ambassadors
have welcomed them
because everybody in this bed
loves everybody else in this bed.

I'm so tired.
I'm so happily dead tired.
Her arm decorates me,
resting like a standard
draped over an empty box.

In this bed tonight
we fought war,
pollution, genocide, and other
forms of extinction.
Tonight we formed a unity
against the night that otherwise surrounds us—

one elation,
under God,
feeling invincible
with levity,

just us—
and all.

Ode to the Middle Finger

My first experience
with American sign language.

An international phenomenon:
The English use two fingers
which is really just the middle finger
with his angry buddy—
and how they create a new English
Channel between themselves—

My grandmother was the one
who taught me how to give the finger properly,
Jersey girl that she was.
My father said her finger was the state bird,
spotted up and down the Parkway
throughout the summer.

She sat me on her lap
and said someday the world
will erode me completely,
although it happens slowly—

She said there are agents of the world's acid
that cut one off in traffic
or tell you that unjust wars are just.

She said to force that acid
through the arm—
let it ball up in a tight fist—

raise that fleshy wrecking ball high above you—

let it become a ship full of your displeasure,
steered by reprobates,
floating past the edge of your tolerance—

then, my grandmother said, raise the main mast—
hoist the skull and crossbones up it.

As a man now, I have come to realize
how her fingernail was a little polished mirror
she held up to the Medusa world,
hoping to punish it with its own ugliness—

And I wish I could go back to Thanksgiving 1978,
when she first taught me how to give the finger,
to tell her thanks,
and to warn her that the fingerprint
facing her
when she flashed her prolific digit
would one day become a whirlpool
dragging her down
into the world's anger.

That's okay, Grandma would have said.
You'll know yourself one day, my love:
nobody floats forever.
On your way down,
sing the world your sign language siren song.
Tell it you know what it's been up to—
bad world, bad world—
and flashing that one finger
shows how you were willing to fight it alone.

No Job, No Money, No Girlfriend

But I have the red blink of the answering machine
    when I get home—

—as if someone out there knew my phone is a wishing well
    and dropped an infrared coin into it—

—a small glinting drop of the warm blood
    that flashed through my circuitry while I was gone—

—a wink from the eye of the junk man when he knows
    he has just the right part to fix what's broke—

—welcome tiny pulsing heart of an opera diva
    (waiting for me to touch her body before she sings)—

—hello little ambulance saying *hello* to me,
    flashing across the dead city of my living room,
    arriving with the hope to revive my etiolated hopes—

—o I swear there is this happy woman dancing in my house,
    lifting and dropping her empire-waisted glad rags with one hand,
    flashing her red fan with the other!—

(When I press the button,

a single electronic static train,
its boxcars full of emptiness,
departs from the speaker,
routes through my chest,
and out the front door—

click

giving me another hang-up.)

To the Turtle

O Original Winnebago—
Sluggish juggernaut of bog—
Only defensive back on the field—
You are not too slow—
This world is too fast—

Brother of All Things Reticent—
                           :O: Mud Dude—
Better to stay in your hemisphere.
Dare you share the map to there?
I stop my errands and study
The longitude and latitude
Markings, that fretwork
Fritted across your rocky,
Charted, old world body.

To the Pussycat

From ragbag, stumblebum, peripatetic lout
To bonfire of catnip that burns itself out—

Bristled sack of hiss & claws
Cinched at the maw—

Other times a wilting in the sun;
A warhead at Yalta; a dreaming nun.

Yet one walled mouse bustle stirs your muscles
Into an under-fur hurricane flinging corpuscles.

Then you curl on the couch, a furry whirlpool
Pulling itself into a dogless world. You'll

Translate milk to purr, a distant thunder
Rumbling over your Teton ears—

Your one life makes mine
Feel fuller, feline, by nine.

Wolverine the X-Man Kisses

His bones, lined with adamantium, are unbreakable,
    so his lover is just licorice and moth wings
in his careful palms.

And tucked within each open hand
    lie three knives retracted,
but one thrust and *snickt*

                                 x, x, x)

whatever he holds could die.
    What delicacy is in his hug,
but is this a fair relationship?

Before you answer, know this:
    he is a mutant, able to heal
from the deepest of cuts,

and so to hurt him
    she must kiss him.
Look at his trembling lips

as he leans in to hers—see the nervous animal
    in his eyes, how it paces back and forth *(x, x, x)*
knowing there is no way out of love

but to suffer. He's a mutant, but is he so different
    from you? Have you ever folded yourself
into someone's arms, unsure of yourself,

knowing what you have learned in your life
    contradicted such tenderness, leaning in anyway,
lips separating, closing in,

the potential of blades
    running along your bones
just in case?

Bruce Springsteen and Jimmy Vivino Jam
at Convention Hall, Asbury Park

Their guitars trade licks like compliments,
then punches,
and the horns scurry
to keep up, one family
scrambling to pay the rent.
Max catches on and tumbles
a charging rhinoceros's heartbeat
into the mix.
Everyone is seriously playing
when Ed Manion's fingers
climb up the neck of his sax
as if they were the four limbs
of some musical King Kong
ascending the Empire State Building
where it will finally mount
and scream out to the dark city
that had once caged it.

And just as I feel this room
can't fit any more boogie in it,
Mark Pender loads his trumpet
with air and fires his volley of notes.
Everyone around me gets hit
and becomes more alive.
And recessed from the proscenium,
there's Mike Spengler, his hair
slicked back like Dracula's,

his trumpet sucking all the blood
from the guitars and turning it
into good cholesterol.
Then Jerry Vivino juts forth
his saxophone like he's got a crush
on this audience
and he's offering a brassy petunia,
its reedy stem full of *carpe noctem*
in this greenhouse of sound—

just a ramshackle theatre
on the edge of a city of ruins
near an ocean that incessantly loses
its tug-of-war with the resolute land,
but the water never gives up—

and LaBamba gets it—
his trombone starts flicking out
like Sugar Ray Robinson's jab—
a pounding and an exaltation at once—
and we audience—we start clapping
on the beat, and Max the drummer smiles
like we're patting his back.
We slam our palms together
as if capturing some indestructible fireflies—
each one's wings a set
of humming stereophonic speakers.
How we want to bring them home with us.
We want evidence of such life on this planet.
We keep clapping the air in front of us.

At the Party: "So What Do You Do?"

I say I'm an electrician
trying to connect the wires of the alphabet—

or a non-profit whiskey maker,
distilling to disquiet—
making myself giddy on sounds—
arranging a concert on the page
with a 26-piece band
the world is invited to—

or that Creation sometimes talks to me
and I try to build an ark of ink
that my fellow creatures
might find themselves in—

an admirable admiral animal—

I try to brew it
so that a shock of pleasure
floats through it.

Development

(Walking the new K. Hovnanian Property in northwest Jersey)

In that house I built
a bonfire that illuminated
the fecund earth around it.
And in that split-level
my friend Tommy, only eight
teeth left in his whole head,
dug a huge illegal grave
to bury his father's packhorse.
He marched that sumpter
into the dark study
and shot its head on the left
so it would fall right.
That night, as if to argue
with the day,
Karen and I made love
on the front lawn of the mansion
one cul-de-sac down,
four feet away
from what would be
a window cracked
open to allow the outside
in.

But the houses
were just fields then.
And we were wild.

Cross-Pollination

My favorite cross-pollination
is the one between Shakespearean English
and Jersey City English—

This particular breed of language
has trouble surviving modern airs—
but recalcitrantly remains
in one final saying:

I shit you not.

Such mellifluous wings
skirting inches above a manure field.

It means, "I do not shit you—"
yet no one says that.
If one were to say it,
we'd expect a head shake
or social shunning.

But "I shit you not"
implies that the speaker
is fairly well-read
and, furthermore, is not prevaricating
about the matter at hand.

My favorite instance of it
came when I was told that
my old boss, who fired me,
was fired for being a lousy boss.

Bradford called me up and said,
"Ward—he was fired!
I shit you not."

Or my mother—
telling me an acceptance letter arrived from a college—
saying, "You got in. I shit you not."

Or Gretchen Honecker,
in the late 20th century parking lot of the White Castle,
telling me, "I love you."
I, a bigger fool then than I am now,
said, "Really?"
And she leaned close to my ear
and whispered,
"I shit you not...."

The saying is a nail
driving through disbelief,
expelling dismissal,
pealing *yes, amen,* nod nod nod,
and tacking a friend's voice
to one of those rare moments in life
one would never get rid of.

Shotgun Wedding 2006

Getting married ½ an hour before traffic
court began,
people thought we were speeding—
not our mothers and fathers,
there to witness
the joy cemented into the place it grew—

but rather the eyebrow raisers & sibilance dwellers—
    She's pregnant, it's hiss—   hiss—

Our son, four months in your belly
and already smarter than the President,
just lay there and grew quietly
as our marriage became
the second product of our love.

Judge Palmer asked,
        in his dry legal way,
"Do you love her with a part of your
 soul you didn't even know about until
 you kissed her?"

"I'm guilty of that," I said.
"And do you?" he said.
"I do too," you said.

And then it was like the father
   of us all
pointed a shotgun at me
   and fired joy
through all my organs.

The judge sentenced us to life—
      real, awake life
         out of the jails we had been roaming in—
      life in prism—

then started handing out fines
for parking too long.

We got out of there just in time.

When people say, "That's not very romantic,"
I tell them what's not romantic
   are themselves—
for it was the most beautiful wedding—
   perfect
   because you were there
   and—   O Sweet World—
            you said yes.

Babyproofing

(for Doc Tatu)

A baby sharpens the eye.
You used to try to make the world suffer
but now, Mr. Harley-Davidson,
glance around your nursery
and try to make the world safer.
Be rid of the poker
and shovel your own father
left to you—you could never
build a fire anyway.
The whiskey moves higher
and the dogs get shot
for distemper. Bang
down the nails that have protruded
for as long as you've lived
here. How many nights
you've whetted
edges on knives
you must now move from edges.
Look at that baby
with your jaw, your hands—
you'll have to squeeze hard
to open a door from here
on in.
      You're almost frantic now,
        aren't you Daddy?
                  Here's all
you can do: pick up everyday
objects, then examine them.
Everything might hurt.

Hee Blow

leads to Bear Down—
Bear Down
gives way to little crown—
Crown concedes the Head—
then Head produces All—
Snip the fruity cord—
little King begins to bawl
then grows bored—
So begins his fall—

Book Tour: Another Barnes & Noble—
Empty Chairs and Good Coffee

(for Michael Jemal)

The words I speak to these chairs
must be silencing.
It has stunned them
into a profound emptiness.
No creaking from the gallery—
no James Joyce here, nor Malory—

An unknown author
in a very large chain—

can't you hear me rattling?

Naming the Growth

We're only temporary, then we're crushed.
Botanists, nomenclature-drunk, decreed
"love-in-a-mist" is now "devil-in-the-bush."

Love was such a choice tag. Why the rushed hush?
Can they kill a name? Must science concede
we're only temporary, then we're crushed?

This study of life gestates so much fuss—
to call a single plant from one lone seed
"love-in-a-mist," then "devil-in-the-bush"—

But names mirror the namer's state: a plush
romance, or decay heartbreak breeds, then feeds
(Pain avers we're temporary, then crushed).

A love that's lush is grand until we're touched
by grief and secede. Hindsight renames deeds:
love-in-a-mist's now devil-in-the-bush.

And you and I, my dear—were we ambushed?
The passion, then fighting—our exeunt a stampede.
We were temporary—then we were crushed.
Love- *(love)* -in-a-mist *(love)* was devil-in-the-bush.

The Photographer's Divorce

She walks out the door for the final time
and her absence is already moving in, clutching
its baggage, looking for whiskey in his cupboard,
negatives in his camera.
Her absence sets the table for one
where it and the man will dine
alone together for many nights.
As they eat each night
in the stark light of a single
candle (how could flame be so cold?),
the absence's shadow flattens out
across the walls he and she once painted together,
leaves a film that thickens his house,
aggregately closing the space he lives in
like a constricting automatic
camera lens
attempting to photograph an object
or occurrence
to which he's too close to see clearly.

It's focusing and focusing
not able to get it—
it focuses so hard
it pulls the garden into the house,
and then the street—
after that, a mountain, a few distant clouds—

soon the whole world
is something he can't see
as it crowds his house.
In fact, everything is now in his house
except her.

When I Submitted "Stopping by Woods on a Snowy Evening" to My Workshop

Finally someone asks, "Why is he out there?"
upon which three "I don't know"s
and one "Un-Hunh" flourish around the classroom.
"Well, it's ... nice," says one woman,
who says that about any poem
when there are more than ten seconds of silence in the room.
Then the man who loves to wear spandex says,
"This house—in the village—it's not very specific,"
and everyone nods, and "Tell us what color it is" is offered
by the retired school nurse whose poems
are always about administering Ritalin.
Then the Salem man, whose face
should be the "before" model for sleeping pills,
blurts out, "Wait! This guy is into bestiality!"
and the woman who thought it was "nice"
blushes and seems about to faint.
Sleepless in Salem continues, "The horse! The horse
is giving his harness bells a shake—
he's refusing the writer!"
"You mean the narrator," admonishes the workshop leader.
"Yes," confirms the tie–dyed cheese-maker
who's bitter about anything published
that's not bound by staples.
"That's why they've stopped without a farmhouse near."
Then the always-stoned nineteen-year-old chimes in,
"And those harness bells are a-shakin', baby!"
And they all laugh and then they all stop
and look at me and for a moment
I think maybe I'm a pervert

and I look back at them
and they all quickly turn back to the page
and silence sets in again when—sweet
redemption—the only writer I trust in the class says,
"Wait—you've all got it wrong,"
but then he continues,
"It says right here, 'My little horse must think I'm queer.'"
"It's queer!" I blurt. "It's queer!"
and everyone gets mad at me for breaking the no-talking rule.
Then the flurry of questions: "Exactly how do woods
fill up with snow? Is that possible?"
and "What's the calendar date
of the darkest evening of the year?"
Then the performance poet, who has exactly ten expletives
in every poem, matching the number of tattoos on his body,
says, "Yo yo yo—What promises does my boy have to keep?
'Tain't clear. Dat's all I'm sayin'. Just keepin' it real yo …"
and again the "It's-all-Greek-to-me" chorus of "Un-Hunh"s
re-experiences its song of ignorance.
The scowling PETA woman who berated me the first class
for wearing a wool sweater mutters almost inaudibly,
"He sure isn't worried about that horse."
Then the man who smells every night like he just cooked
a whole feast made of garlic, leeks, and masala
and who muses weekly about his frustrated love life
asks, "What about the last two lines?"
The leader replies, "Redundant,"
then adds, "Anything else about this poem?"
Spandex man pipes in, "Why is he so tired?"

Upon Being Asked about the Importance of Context

Advice for the Groom:

For the rest of your life,
you best be conscious of your wife.

Be sure to always get her back.

Advice for the Cuckold:

For the rest of your life,
you best be conscious of your wife.

Be sure to always get her back.

Portrait of the Artist as Egg Salad

I am writing this poem
while my fingers smell like egg salad.
You are reading this poem
on paper that, I'm fairly sure,
doesn't smell like egg salad
because publishers don't use that kind of paper
anymore. Now you know a little
about my world, I about yours.
But it's not the egg salad
I'm trying to convey—it's how
replete my sandwich is—toasted
whole wheat, red leaf lettuce, a slice
of Jersey tomato. But I'm sure
you can't taste it, though I sure can,
and I am reminded of the thickest-

headed student I ever had—Debra—
who, when I told her her poem conveyed
nothing, said, "But I really feel this."

So here we are,
Debra invoked yet long gone,
just writer and reader liaising
in the rectangular dining room of the page,
me still eating my egg salad sandwich,
you beginning to cross your arms and get upset

because I haven't offered you anything yet
and you're still hungry and it's all my fault.

The Closer

What leaf-fringed legend haunts about thy shape … What wild ecstasy …
—John Keats

The hinge of an empire
        is a right elbow.

One cannot count how many grins habited the bleachers
when a lumbering slugsmith or feckless swatsman
    supposed to make a bat
        slap a ball
couldn't purchase a single with his million dollar paycheck.

How many times I witnessed some hungry lumber
    try to take a chomp of the hot meal
only to splinter into a father, a son,
    and the Paraclete of the white ball,
its sutures still bloody from that operation,

rolling easily toward sure-handed Jeter—
    himself all vac-u-matic torque twisting from a pair of cleats—
who'd scoop and spin like a sudden dust devil in shallow left,
    rubbernecking as if some vulpine beauty were at first
        (too bad it was only Jason Giambi)—

and deliver it to the mitt's court
    like it was fresh-pressed law
sent forth from a minor god on a 10″ mountain—
    the tablets of the scoreboard forever etched with the news.

Cuckoldom

Such conundrums
of English. I blame
my ex-wife. She
rearranged my
dictionary, or re-
taught an old story:
in this book,
if you look
for alimony,
it follows
acrimony (nothing
between). However,
contrition still
borders contrivance
(if it can be seen).
Untruth in her
troth sallowed
the language, sullied
a certain conjugation:
how she lied
as she lay with me.
Apparently her
monogamy was too
close to monotony.

Alas, after parting
with that particular
lass, I remain
a student
examining all
our words'
gradation:
how anniversary
now precedes
annihilation.

Jack & Jill

That's what they called it—"fetching a pail of water"—when they went to Point Mountain to make out as the sun lay down beneath the far, argent edge of the earth's bedspread, shooting its rays up through the barest threads, creating some celestial mood lighting as Jack and Jill got it on.

For these two high school students, each other's mouth became a vast new world with its own time zones and valleys they loved getting lost in. They kissed awhile, then Jack said, "Want to try something different?" Jill smiled, something Jack knew as her quiet "yes," as if her lips had an aboriginal language and he was their only countryman. For Jack, it was all call-and-response.

He produced a pint bottle of Crown Royal. From another mountaintop, it might have looked like an arsonist holding some gas, but one could not tell if she were the co-conspirator or the church that would get burnt down. What happened was this—he puckered his lips and pulled from the bottle and then she and then he and then she again, more boldly this time.

And they kissed and pulled and kissed and felt and groped and kissed and pulled. Jack stood up, looked out at the half-sun on the horizon, its halo cryptic and, he thought, romantic. Maybe even redeeming. Now the clouds seemed drunk like him, stumbling over the sky. The wind sloshed in the trees and through everything he heard Jill say, "Come back, Jack." And to him, she was the exposure of all latent beauty.

In years, he'd stop feeling this—resign himself to commuter trains and a mortgage with a wife he hasn't yet met. But this was Jack and Jill, on top of the hill, and she wanted to fetch more water. The whiskey and Jill's eyes seemed to fill Jack with the entire sky, the entire business, and the only way to let any of it out was to howl, which he did, and then Jill stood up laughing to hug him on top of the darkening mountain, their youth fading away like the eastern landscape. Soon it would be hard to remember what it looked like. But they were swigging now and shrieking and then Jack fell down and broke the glass bottle and Jill—

Jill came tumbling after.

Ars Poetica

The 39-year-old hand-transplant Frenchman
    gave advice
to the 38-year-old face-transplant Frenchwoman:

"This is not who you are," he said
    as he grazed her face
with his acquired hand.

"And this is not who I am."
    He then felt
transported when he gazed at her original eyes

beneath someone else's eyelashes, eyebrows,
    collapsed-upwards eyelids …
"Oui," she said.

And, dear stranger, this is not my poetry
    (which is what uses language as a sleeve).
It is the ink that obstructs it.

These words are my mother's,
    my father's, my brother's, my lender's, my garbage
man's—the poem runs

like oil on fire
    beneath this earth where we know each other.
Witness the black smoke everywhere.

Compassion

Out in this profane city,
sometimes sidewalks
seem the only cement that connects us,
pressed by the sacred strangers
we will never touch.
Everyone's ribs are scaffolding
around the shabby, gleaming
opera houses of their hearts—
scaffolding
because so many urban hearts
are in a constant state of repair.

You're in your
big rent little apartment,
appearing to sip tea
but really checking your scars
which spell your real name.

So many productions
have played out in you,
sometimes you can't believe you're alive.
Sometimes you can.
And through these shows,
compassion has endured
in its orchestra pit,
with a violin shaking in its tenacious fingers.

In your body's travels,
who knows what
makes compassion scratch out
its mercy to some other being.
Your tea still steams.
The curtains rise like ghosts
of neighbors no longer there.
The man in the street
is down there—
the pocked, destitute one
with lips like railroad tracks
from the cold—
the city's windows' light
no source of warmth.

You ponder what craziness
compelled you to do that—
made your hand rise
as if you were a strings conductor
in the pregnancy of silence
before the first note
corrals the entire house
to the millimeter
where a stretched strand
touches another stretched strand.
You ponder the buck
you then pressed
into that unknown man's hand
simply because he asked you for money.

He'll spend it on booze,
people will say.
You're stupid, they'll spit.
He'll spend it on his
own death, they'll chide.
Who doesn't? you'll rejoin.
That man many stories below
now slumps against a fence,
our first President's face
shoved into the delicate crease
where his filthy hip hinges with his lame leg.

You're a bill poorer but your inner
walls feel emblazoned by a song
rising from fathomless depths,
a rosined bow rubbing
its awfully taut body
against catgut

to make music.

Resurrection

Well after Darwin
and Freud, my grown
children groan
God's dead—
that faith's a fraud.
That's what they said.
       Yet their
answer to the galaxies'
mysteries suddenly
seemed specious to them
when their friend
inexplicably got cancer
and died.
      Dismayed,
they prayed. They
hoped to believe
when they grieved.
      Now it's Easter—
and I'm wondering
about our first blunder:
was Original Sin
Yahweh's win-win?
Was the apple cause
for angels' thundering
applause? Did Eve turn
to Adam knowing the globe
had him, pause, then whisper,

before the little, potent feast,
there among the non-
threatening beasts, *"Bite the apple.*
We'll construct a chapel—"?

The kids' friend is dead and
the dead resurrected God,
or at least a faint belief
(which ain't faith, they say).
We sit in a circle—a family
semi-corrected—and thank
different things, then carve
an animal. Now, two beings
will be missing, both feeding
us somehow. The garden salad
seems seminal. My son
says he's starved. We uncover
what grew, then ask for dressing.

"And All the Peasants Cheered for the King. The End."

I close the storybook and my son looks up.
He is swaddled with a bravery he knows nothing about:
    Astronauts floating across his pajamas—
    Soldiers bivouacking on his bookshelf—
    Knights on his lamp—so that his light
        shines right through armor.

"What's a peasant, Daddy?"
I don't think much of the answer: "A poor person."
"Like Grandma and Grandpa?"

And now the story is personal.

My son plays on the junkers my father works on forever—
the front yard is Grandpa's cold scriptoria
and he writes everything in blue collar serifs,
spending his days off rendering metal
into combustion.
Henry Ford invented the printing press
that churned out his Bible.

And my mother with her three shirts that fit—
her Bayonne accent a Cockney in my son's suburban world.

When I lend my parents money, that word has to be used—
lend—or else they wouldn't take it. Even poor people
have Pride as a lawyer.

I was his age when I first knew we were poor.
"Are we poor?" I had asked my mother.
Her eyes were just beginning
their descent deeper into her beauty—
they may have begun
to run away from the world just then,
at her older son's question—

"No," her mouth said, as obviously as possible.

Her hand stroked my hair.
It said, *I'm erasing that question.*

Her tremble said, *Yesterday my boss
held an empty wallet to my head.*

But were we rich somehow?
C'mon—you know the clichés.
But were we rich in another way?

My father knows how to make stillness move.
At the Foodtown, the cashiers always smiled,
for my mother was an S&H Green Stamp magnate.
My brother and I learned how to love
without dropping our eyes
below the neck.
If money's king, my family served it well.
We only asked to be able to sleep through the night.

And now, my own son is looking up at me,
seeing something he doesn't recognize.
I tell him, "Peasants live in kingdoms,"
and shut out the light—

The astronauts are still fastened in their flotation.
The soldiers still guard the fairytales.

After Googling Myself, I Pour Myself Some Scotch and Step Out onto My Front Porch

As it turns out, I'm not B.J. Ward.

According to the search engine,
she's an opera diva who could pack the Met
and palms a good bit of side cash
for being Velma on *Scooby-Doo*
and giving voice to Smurfs.

If more than twenty people show up for my reading,
I know they want B.J. Ward the mystery-solving Smurf opera singer,
not BJ Ward the waitress's son.

I have nothing but duct-taped syntax to offer them—
noise of jury-rigged verse, of entire days burned
by the focus of a foreman's glare, the labored breath
of an exhausted ride home
while she sings in a tiara and cape
to tuxedoed men and bespangled women.
Yet the world sounds most honest to me
when its timing chain is slightly off.
How it revs, how it almost sputters out
on any given evening after a long day of work.

My neighbors' houses abound around me
like Stonehenge wannabees.
Their antennas—already antiquated—rise
like our culture's dipsticks
checking the universe's oil—
it's all dry, but somehow
the cosmos' engine keeps turning
over above me.

Will archaeologists 10,000 years from now
study our neighborhoods to determine
the precise ratio of possessions to happiness,
or lack thereof?
I read these houses like a sweatpantsed augur:
work your ass off all day
so you have a place to park your ass-nub at night.
And on nights like this, I feel like a sparkplug
looking up at the engine
that discarded me.
I just didn't conduct properly,
it all says.

I smell how the trees
are in full throttle,
broadcasting their good exhaust.
I don't know my neighbors, Paul and a woman
who renamed herself Karma.
And they don't know me
because I don't even know me.

How could we know our own cornucopian hearts?
My heart is fathomless
and it's always flirting with me.
I fear I've begun to learn to ignore it.

I'm not B.J. Ward anymore.
Even Google can't find that me.
The landlord knocking on the door used to be my tympani,
but lately it's the memory
of my baby's heartbeat
on that first Ultrasound,
and how I now hold up his perfect chest to my ear
every night before putting him down
as if recalibrating myself to love's syncopation
and then I can get up tomorrow and face the 21st century again.

What a sum freedom plus apathy have equaled.
I swirl my snifter of scotch on the rocks
like a combustive New Year's Eve noisemaker—
tinkle tinkle little pop.
An owl spills out of the rucksack of stars
and lands in Karma's manicured elm,
then accuses all of us anonymous neighbors.
He's an original search engine.
And now another:
a car full of hooting teenagers howls by.
I remember being in that car—
all that high school tension
released in the rev of an engine.

I toast it. I toast them and then I toast the owl.
I toast all the starlight getting closer
even if the engines have since died,
and the moon moving away from us
about a centimeter every year,
and all the other strained marriages I know of,
and I toast the line that stops some wives from calling
their husbands "frenemies,"
and the dark oil that keeps the universe turning.
I toast all the teachers who warned me
about selling happiness for a buck
and the younger me who didn't know
he didn't know.
I toast everything until I myself
am toasted.

My younger self is dead now.
He's been pulled from the hot rod
and buried in my perfect lawn.
Scott's Turf Guard prints the eulogy everyday
in the barcodes on its hermetic bags.
I built the back deck over him.
My wife still loves him
and tries to resurrect him in the bedroom.
My son won't believe he ever existed.

Is this what earnings earn?
Am I celebrating or am I mourning
with this scotch? I toast all the engines

I never controlled—even in the bellies
of these lightning bugs,
which float over my lawn as if
experiencing some viscosity.
I wonder how many of them
are plagiarizing their patterns of light.
I wonder how many others are lighting up
for the first time tonight.
I reckon some mysteries I'll never solve,
but I swear they time it naturally
so a fireworks display
illuminates my property
every 16 seconds—
like a hundred little funeral pyres—
or like a dependence celebration
of a tiny, formerly insular nation
that finally got it right.

Turn up the backfiring. Turn up the rusty hinge.
Turn down the obsequious admiring
that makes the tombgrass cringe.
What the hammer—what the chain—
What's that dread grasp still trying to gain?
What was my landlord building banging
on the door like that? His music's scheming
with rush hour's long refrain—
What beast do we sing to sleep? What large cat?
My mother's face: a deep beauty gleaming
with its constellation of sweat pearled—
Two eggs over easy—Want fries with that?

My fist is her flag still furled.
Take the cannoli and leave the tuxedo—
This is my jackleg opera to the world.
Shooby-dooby-do—Hey Smurf—
Scooby-dooby-don't be so blue.
I'm not B.J. Ward.
How do you do?

GRAVEDIGGER'S BIRTHDAY
(2002)

The longer you live
the sooner you'll bloody well die.

—from "Isn't It Grand," traditional Irish song,
   as sung by Tommy Makem and the Clancy Brothers

Has this fellow no feeling of his business, that he sings
   at grave-making?

—from *Hamlet* (V.i.73), William Shakespeare

We even flew a little.

—from "A Pity. We Were Such a Good Invention,"
   Yehuda Amichai (translated by Assia Gutmann)

The Star-Ledger

287 was the long road to the newspaper plant
    my black-handed father would ride beneath
the weight of a night sky.
    A father who works the night shift
knows that weight, how it accumulates from within
    when his mistakes and debt
begin to press on his children and wife.
    And so went his life—

If the stars spelled something real,
    they might spell the equation
that my father never mastered—
    the news just ran through his hands
and what slid there left the black residue
    of the world's doings, pressed knowledge
that read like misaligned tea leaves in his hardening palms,
    and in his life line and heart line and other lines
that would normally speak a fortune,
    the night just accumulated itself—
a little sky he would spread over us
    when the world redelivered him in the morning.

Gravedigger's Birthday

We had only dated for three weeks
but there I was, burying her cat.
To top things off, it was my birthday,
but I knew the cat's death trumped it
so into the ground I went,
never having dug a grave before
but knowing I should know how.
Such an ancient, simple action,
as if our bodies evolved to do such work—
opposable thumb to dig and dig
deeper into the earth, and standing erect
to toss soil from our graves. I remembered
something from somewhere—boy scouts
or horror movie—delve deep enough
so raccoons can't stir up the corpse.
I did it all quietly with a sudden solemnity
not for the cat—I barely knew it—
but for the motion, the first ancestral thing
I had done in years, aware this was traffic
with old gods. The indifferent stars pinned
the lips of the grave open, and I lifted up
that solid eggplant of a body, and lowered her
carefully into the soil, as if the cat could feel it,
or the earth could. Ridiculous.
Then I lifted up that shovel, again
knowing what to do—load upon load
into the earth, back onto that body,
returning it but also casting it out
of my modern life where I would soon take
the short walk from the grave to the house,

eat some meat without thinking
of eating the meat, get in bed
next to my new, warm, mourning girlfriend
on a mattress imported from far away, some speck
of the grave's dirt rising behind a fingernail
as I lie awake, the faint next click
of my life's odometer there in the darkness,
living and dying at the same time,
thinking how so much motion and instinct
lies inert in the earth next to the swing set,
and how the ground's new toothless mouth
settled into closure without pomp,
temporary and permanent at once.

Education

When Mary and I finally decided we were old
    enough to make love, we needed to find a spot
to park the Datsun.
    Two high school students, we were full
of what the world had not yet offered us.
    Achievement's taste constantly dissolved
under our barely used tongues.
    We approached our old grammar school—
its parking lot spread out
    like an asphalt puddle that had leaked
from the foundation of our early education,
    hardening into something we could anchor on.
We coupled there, the school rising
    above the shifting car. We were lost
in the universe contained in a Datsun—
    everything we had ever learned
was an opaque wall we hid behind
    as we embraced the greatest lesson
there were no instructions for,
    only blanks to fill in
as we discovered them, no wrong answers
    in the multiple choices,
feeling both lost and found at once—we
    were each Columbus, each the other's New World.
Our transmission hovered
    over a hopscotch outline,
the slight chalk markings
    that had once told us where to go,
where not to. It would be years
    before I knew what I learned.

Emperor

I was eighteen. The Garden State Parkway.
The police car in the bushes of the median,
its red light bar like an eyelid suddenly
opening, six eyes flashing about wildly,
looking for me.

"It's an ambush," I thought.
Me, who had my whole empire
in control—even the hairs on my head
were soldiers standing in order, helping me conquer
what I thought I had to own.

I was eighteen. The gas pedal was like all
physical things, destined to fall downward.
And now I confess
I don't remember anything
about the ticket—its cost or the cop

whose hand wrote my birth name
in the tiny squares, incorporating
my identity into the system.
In years I'd know he was just
doing what he had to do—as was I.

"Here's your ticket," he said,
 as if he were an usher
whose job was to rip things in half.
"What am I entering?" I thought.
So my empire began to fall on a shoulder

of the Garden State Parkway—
not usurped, really, but undermined.
I was eighteen and falling
through society's turnstiles—
college, speed limits, combing my hair

into a daily unnoticeable—
a work of art whose strength
was that it didn't particularly stand out,
like driving well. I drove off,
pushing the accelerator pedal

to the exact angle of, say,
the Tower of Pisa.
How I wanted to topple it.
How it became the only thing in my world
that could ever rise back.

Spring Begins in Hinckley, Ohio

For the past 41 years, the town of Hinckley, Ohio, has waited patiently for what it considers the first true indication that spring is here—the return of the buzzards. For four decades now, a flock of buzzards—also known as turkey vultures—returns each March 15 to Hinckley's rocky ledges. And this year, despite a blowing snow and sub-freezing temperatures, the buzzards did not disappoint.
                    —CNN (March 15, 1998)

I

I am sure the axis of the earth
passes through Hinckley, Ohio,
because every year the buzzards drop down—
little flags of death
lowered on an ancient flagpole—
and people rejoice.
The town runs out of champagne.
How appropriate to cherish
the reinstated balance of the world—
vultures corkscrewing down as tulips squeeze
themselves open—a wrenching into tenderness—
and spring herself starts teasing out the grasses,
tuning up the wind's motor, airing out the willows' drapes,
setting up summer's bright, unlocked house.
And with life rising and eternity dropping,
Hinckley's people become suddenly and quite happily caught again
between a contralto and baritone singing the same song.

II

I am east of Hinckley—northwestern New Jersey,
where for some reason the world is still still
and warmth is a love letter on the way
via bulk rate. However, the teethed cold
outside the car can't keep this sky from blushing
as I ride partially into it, partially out of it.
Here everything outdoors is locked frozen,
but what compels me are the worms
deep beneath the ice—those puny and insistent ground vultures,
little squirming letters that spell a frightening word—
the worms who have been eating decayed
hands, buried waste, swallowing dog turds
as if they were éclairs. To have that hunger for waste—
to blindly eat the rusting rainbow taffeta
of last year's leaves.... I love how they love
what is used and then spoiled—how they, deep
in their wormy brains, must know that death is a factory
always in production, always in the black,
and how they set up their pantry there,
beneath the cold, immersed in the earth
where we'll all return when we are done
driving, done waitressing or practicing law,
done with grieving and done with loving
what is passing, done with eating whatever
death we eat and justify with our own vulture logic.

III

People of Hinckley celebrate one thing in two halves:
while the world opens its wide garage doors again
to thoughts of rebirth, bumper crops, and long summer kisses,
above and below us there is an ancestral motion
scribbling its uneasy language
against the sky and in the earth,
                        its ancient hand slowly spelling, as if in no rush,
Bring it all back through my body.

Daily Grind

A man awakes every morning
and instead of reading the newspaper
reads Act V of *Othello*.
He sips his coffee and is content
that this is the news he needs
as his wife looks on helplessly.
The first week she thought it a phase,
his reading this and glaring at her throughout,
the first month an obsession,
the first year a quirkiness in his character,
and now it's just normal behavior,
this mood setting in over the sliced bananas,
so she tries to make herself beautiful
to appease his drastic taste.
And every morning, as he shaves
the stubble from his face, he questions everything—
his employees, his best friend's loyalty,
the women in his wife's canasta club,
and most especially the wife herself
as she puts on lipstick in the mirror next to him
just before he leaves. This is how he begins
each day of his life—as he tightens the tie
around his neck, he remembers the ending,
goes over it word by word in his head,
the complex drama of his every morning
always unfolded on the kitchen table,
a secret Iago come to light with every sunrise
breaking through his window, the syllables
of betrayal and suicide always echoing
as he waits for his car pool, just under his lips
even as he pecks his wife goodbye.

Roy Orbison's Last Three Notes

12 mph over the speed limit on Route 80, I realize
the way I know the exact size of my bones
is the way I know I am the only one
in America listening to Roy Orbison
singing "Blue Bayou" at this precise moment,
and I feel sorry for everyone else.
Do they realize they are missing
his third from last note?—*Bluuuueee*—
and how it becomes a giant mouth I'm driving into—
"Bay"—pronounced *bi*—becomes the finger
pointing back—*biiiiiii*—and all the sealed-up cars
greasing along this dirty, pot-holed clavicle of New Jersey
don't know this "you"—constant as my exhaust smoke—
yooooouuuu—and the beats underneath, more insistent
than the landlord knocking on the door—horns, drums, guitar, bass—
my Toyota Corolla is now one serious vehicle,
and the band and I are all alone now, filling it up—
Roy and me in our cool sunglasses up front
and his musicians barely fitting their instruments in the back,
driving into the blue—bom bom bom—pulling ahead
of the pollution faster than New Jersey can spit it out—
Bye—boom bom—his leggy background singers must be jammed
in the trunk because suddenly I hear them and suddenly
we are Odysseus and his boys bringing the Sirens with us,
and the cassette player is our black box
containing all essential details in case we don't make it,

but I know we're going to make it
because Roy Orbison turns to me
and says, like the President says to his top general
after a war has been won, or like Morgan Earp
on his deathbed said to Wyatt when vengeance
was up to him, or like Gretchen Honecker
said when I knew I was about to get my first kiss,
Roy turns to me and says, "*You*—"

Christmas Eve, 1975: What I Realize Now

I: *My Mother, the Waitress: The 3 to 11 Shift*

The repairmen winked at her,
    an executive pinched her ass.
This is how her tips grew large

all evening long, just as the savings
    had grown large for our gifts—
the savings that Father blew on gin & Bud

a little every day in November
    until only zeroes were left
for her eyes. She was working to buy

a watch for me, a horn for Tiny, Rock 'Em Sock 'Em
    for both of us. If she could pull
30 more dollars she could get these three gifts

and the K-Mart was open till midnight.
    She was doing all sorts of shifts
to make everyone happy.

It was love, Christmas, and love
    was something we learned from Mother.
We learned Christmas from Mom.

II: *My Father: Out of Beer, It Must Be Our Fault*

It was love, Christmas, and love
　　rained down from stars
as Father's hands rained on us.

His fist was cold and constructed
　　over years of labor—his breath was death
and, this being Christmas Eve, death was what he celebrated

in his own fatherly ways. He smashed
　　himself into liquor and then smashed
that liquor into us. I ran

through the den, the din
　　following, almost engulfing me.
Tiny hid beneath the tree,

the lights blinking a wild electricity,
　　circuits clicking, my father reaching
beneath the ornaments, unwrapping

his belt. There beneath the mistletoe
　　the buckle kissed my brother's cheek
and I yelled to hell with Christmas

and shoved the tree over. Father chased,
    stumbled, and my brother and I burst
through the door like wounded deer,

darting into the cold snow and unknown
    presents the dark offered. But no—
it wasn't dark. We had each other,

and we ran through starlight.

III: *My Brother and I: Clearing the Stream*

The drainage pipe was clogged with autumn–
        worn debris & leaves and held
our stream with this ugly, thick tongue.

We started tugging, pulling handfuls of dead
        wood from our water, which we needed to clear.
Our father was drunk, violent, and yelling

for us. His voice echoed in the dark woods.
        Hand over hand we yanked a hole
through the accumulations of a hard fall,

each encouraging the other, saying,
        We can't get hurt. It's Christmas Eve,
while our hands froze with each plunge

into garbage. Once the water was freed,
        we could hide in the safe, cold pipe,
whose only echoes would be ours.

When Mother arrived home, her pockets emptied
        but hands full of the three gifts
she stumbled over something in the living room.

Father was passed out, using the fallen tree
    as a pillow, belt still in hand. She waited
all night for us, afraid to call the police,

not knowing we were shivering in the pipe,
    the echoes still looming about us,
blow-down zones in our eyes, and hugging,

giving each other Christmas,
    thinking, if we could wait it out,
how great Christmas morning would be—

there would be the delightful sound of bells,
    an angel's voice maybe.
Maybe just a little quiet after.

Bastards with Badges

A bottle was never more tyrannous
than when smashed against the wall
behind my mother. She left Him,

taking us with her, and for five nights
we slept in the rotting frame of her Chevy Impala,
shipwrecked on the dark shore of the Acme parking lot.

Now Bradford says to me,
"All cops are bastards with badges"—
some acid laced with vanilla truth.

I know how the sense of power could be a siren song
that outseduces the sense of justice, just an ocean
cops float on with its monotonous sounds.

And I know there are no words to describe for Bradford
the precise smell of the Impala's rug
as I lay over the transmission hump

behind the long front seat, my brother tossing
on the vinyl specimen board of the back seat, tossing
in the tidal wave of fear that moved all night through the Chevrolet.

How can I explain to Bradford that there was a cop car
poised at the far end of the lot like a storm waiting to approach—
kept at bay by some invisible high pressure system?

I hated those cops, those salivating hybrids
of sharks and dobermans who faced us all night,
making sure we didn't steal. Everyone knew my family.

How can I explain that they *were* watching us,
some kind of angels with guns, cherry-topped lighthouses
as we drifted across dark, unknown currents—

guardians of the asphalt—for once, we had guardians—
all of us prone in the car, stretched between
locked doors, so far from the darkening sky

that was always in our house, so close
to the driveshaft, for five safe nights—
and I looked at my beautiful mother,

a first mate suddenly forced to be captain
of a ship out of control and already half-wrecked,
my beautiful mother, her sleeping head right

between the steering wheel and gas pedal,
as if her dreams could drive us towards dawn.
The sun eventually smashed through our windows,

glimmering like the sky's shiny new badge.
I surveyed our survival—the cops were gone,
just the three of us lying flat out on our possessions.

Above us all rose my mother's hand, dangling from the column shifter
like some battle-tattered flag for independence, surrounded
by the glass shards and quietude of a parking lot gone empty.

My beautiful mother, safer than ever before,
even in defection. ¼ tank of gas, fully empowered,
her car pointed in every direction.

Upon Being Told Again There Are
No Rhymes for Certain Words

Crossing to my studio eighty yards
through some briars, I lug a verbal freight:
both volumes of the *New Shorter Oxford*
English Dictionary. I contemplate
a carpenter bringing a lumber pile
to his wood shop—I want to build structures
from words that readers could live in awhile.
I know it's rare, tricky stuff, such scripture—
umpteen poets, still no rhymes for purple.
Bonds could beat McGwire and Ruth—but orange?
I'd reconstruct Heaven, or usurp Hell—
write till I swing open like a door hinge.
I arrive—a rogue who'd refurbish town.
I take my pen, begin to nail things down.

The Noises I Make

(for Doug Boyce)

My friend hears me in the shower singing
Tom Waits' "The Piano Has Been Drinking"

at 8:15 a.m. A composer,
he critiques me. "Maybe the tongue throes, or

the timing, or the pitch, the inflections."
I don't care—I rejoice in my imperfections.

I lift my shirt and scratch my belly
for the cause of impropriety.

I snore at night; my lungs are just big toys—
even when I sleep, I make all the wrong noise.

New Jersey

Whenever friends visit from far away—
San Francisco or Jamaica—
what amazes them about my state
more than the long couch of the shore
looking at the constant television of the ocean
or the cloverleaf exit ramps swirling out
like ribbons about to be tightened
on the gift of traffic congestion—
what amazes them are the groundhogs—
"What a noble creature," George said.
"Holy crow, mon, a land seal," said Billson.
And there it is—a stubby, little, near-sighted Buddha
looking up from the county road's bank
as we stop the car, reverse back to it.
If we were all in a bar in Bayonne,
its look would say, "I'm gonna kick your ass."
In a library, it would say, "Why are you
disturbing me? I'm reading Kierkegaard."
But this is the weedy hips of the thoroughfare,
and our friend is mid-sentence in the grass's long summer novel,
navigating its own cloverleaves. It considers us
in our ridiculous car, and then something amazing—
it stands up on its hind legs—and I realize
the Jersey water has helped it evolve
into something more human.

This is New Jersey.
We're crawling on four wheels backwards,
looking at its pinched face,
the shimmering flanks, the dehydrated hands—
the short, imperfect loveliness of groundhog.

After I Read Sandy Zulauf's "Across the Bar,"
Victoria Takes Me Skiing

I don't even like how it looks, Sandy—
the word "skiing"—
with that double i, like twin daggers
jutting from the word's deep pockets
towards me.
Vowels are supposed to be flowing and feminine—
consonants, guttural and male.
But these i's have their own grammar.
There they are—
Victoria would say they look like skis,
your wife Madeline might say ski poles,
but I say they are twin stilettos
that have already killed a consonant
that used to be there.

And I like even less the act itself.
Sandy, guys like us should trudge,
barrel, invade, whack away weeds with machetes—
but Madeline and Victoria tried to get us
to flow, to work easily across this new skin from the sky.
I know what their circular, beautiful
woman logic is saying to them:
that we're poets, we're used
to spreading easily across white surfaces,
making our way from one margin to the other
and leaving marks—

that our tracks are like cursive writings across a field,
the pokings of ski poles
like punctuation that helps us pace.

In short, they tried to kill us, Sandy.
So I offer them this poem,
written in curses and cursive,
and here I think I actually got somewhere,
like the beer that slalomed down my throat
as I watched Victoria finish her skiing,
a skating clef along the musical note tree line,
looking absolutely lovely against the fresh snow
like the perfect word in a poem as you write it—
the trails behind her like the echoes of that word
that remain after you've moved on,
                              a double pleasure,
or perhaps the trails are a double i
flowing behind her pretty legs,
us men just consonants on the outside.

Reloading the Stapler

Little bucktoothed alligator
ready to taste my bills.

Make something suffer.
Make something stick.

Bandages

—One week after my student is raped.

In the hallway while classes were in session
my student quietly confided to me,
shaking like a lake in an earthquake.
She began to break down and in three seconds
moved her hands quickly enough to shield
her face, then chest, then opposite forearms,
as if trying to cover a huge country with body parts,
or the shadows of them. Then she burst
her arms open and threw herself upon me,
murmuring she had only told her two best friends
before me and then her head was buried
in my chest and I put my arms around her
tentatively, looking over her shoulders
to see if anyone could see us. I wanted to shove her
away, thinking of my job, of headlines,
of how this kind of comfort was outside
the behavioral guidelines of my contract.
She began to sob more softly while holding me
tightly, and I let her. I let her have control
of me for that moment. I let her break
behavioral guidelines as more important ones
had been broken on her. And then we stopped
being student and teacher—just a couple people
at a loss when the powerful and unexpected
had been suddenly thrust upon us.
The principal and three students turned the corner
and stopped short. I knew it might be years
before I cleared my name, but far longer

for her to reclaim her life. *"Mr. Ward!"*
from the principal's thick throat, crashing
down the hall, drawing teachers out
just like echoes from their doorways. *Mr. Ward!*
Mr. Ward! I had already closed my eyes
and could smell her hair. Sweet. She had stopped
sobbing and we hugged in silence.
As they drew closer, she tightened
so I did too. We were as quiet and taut as bandages
upon each other. Yes, I squeezed her tighter
as the whole world pressed in on us.

The Suicidologist

He sees in everyone's bodies
the possibility to cast shadows—
finds it so hard
to enjoy himself
at a cocktail party,
all the ladies in their pretty dresses
just covering up some tumult,
some neediness just short of collapsing
into itself.
In the park, on a sunny day at noon,
he looks at all the happy people
standing over the dark spot of themselves
that will surely lengthen
to be bigger than their own bodies
as the day wears itself against them.
As children we learned our shadow
is a darkness we never totally shake
until we lie down, pull the shades,
draw the curtains, shut out the world,
and turn our own light out.

Sunrise, Sunset

Such a bright dark
tune, the chorus reprising
like the celestial cycle itself,
but the song doesn't quite account
for how unstoppably the sunrise barrels
toward us out of the starting gate of the East,
billowing, roiling—an eternally budding fireflower—
and how, after it has incessantly hissed its arias of light
and suffused our gardens with its cargo, soaring overhead
like our earth's nuclear-powered, juggernautish crop-duster
as the austere clouds slide steadfastly across the sky like drunks
trying to maintain their dignity while they escape the last-call flood-
light the bartender has ineluctably switched on, O how the sun
every evening finally settles on the tops of the farthest
western mountains and becomes a fiddler
on a distant neighbor's roof, virtuosic
in the day's final encore, his strings on fire,
and jumps off into the ocean
to put them out.

The 18th Poem

(after Tom Waits)

Small print on a contract
was the ugliest thing you invented.
"I love you" was our pact
in big letters, as if you intended

to honor those words, inhabit that city.
I love you—what else was there to say?
And then your whisper of infidelity—
o how the small print taketh away—

The Poems I Regret in My First Book

Unretractable, obnoxious children
    having tantrums on the dog-eared tabletops
of these pages, screaming out,
    "Failure! Failure!"
in an otherwise classy joint.
    Words I wrote so long ago
while drunk perhaps, or worse, young—
    odious stock that slipped
my editor's eyes, smuggled in, cloaked
    by the good, rightly legal stuff.
A clangorous brood strewn throughout—
    their words are rackety, dull blades—
how they stumble and off the book
    with imprecise cuts.
There they are—irrevocable
    in their deficiencies, the runts of the litter
making the most noise,
    whom I can't punish by banishing
to the room of "Out of Print"
    without sequestering the good children as well.
(This is how books called *Selected Poems* are born.)

So here I am, in front of an audience,
    peddling a volume that should be half-quarantined,
not reading certain pieces,
    keeping those kids on the bench
while about nine players swing for the fence
    and hopefully carry the team.

For Those Who Grew Up on a River

(for Frank Niccoletti)

Brethren of muck and trout—
sultans of pike and pollywog—
clasping ropes that swung over wispy reflections
we'd shatter with our summer bodies.
We look at the world
as one long page
with fluid sentences
running across it.
I remember how the river bebopped
to its own insistent aria,
a motion whose seduction
was challenged only

by Janey's lucid summer dress
which waved to me unbearably.
I left rafts and inner tubes
for Chevies, Plymouths, anything
with a motor to take me
down asphalt estuaries,
Janey at my side,
accelerating toward an ocean
of credit and responsibility.
I felt then
the river was what I'd leave behind,
drift into the world of skyscrapers
and my children's dance lessons.

How hard it was to learn
motors fail. Romance dies.
My river compatriots,
maybe only you understand this:

the more rocks we hit,
the louder we sing.
Janey's long gone.
The river still kisses me.

Filling in the New Address Book

But rifling through the old one,
choosing whom to preserve
in your encyclopedia of associates,
whom to let become obsolete—
no room for them in your entire world.
You little god, you,
you puny pocket of omnipotence—
how you throw people off the side
of your dinghy-book,
a tiny captain thinking, "This is dead weight."
Old girlfriends—doubly gone now.
Old drinking buddies, married and laden
with responsibility, that grand soberer.
So you continue, you infinitesimal infinite one,
scratching out the names of the dead,
people you are coming from and never toward,
tearing down street signs, phone lines,
upheaving entire highways between you
as you leave them out,
their new and unfamiliar lives
not any less full than if you included them.
They are manning their own ships and,
sorry little god,
no room for you on their voyage either.
It's understood, no? How you've been heroes together
in past lives within this life—
Ulysseses now full of uselessnesses—
and why threaten any miraculous history,
any great testament, with knowledge
of how empty your current book of stories is?

My Mother's Last Cigarette

(for His Holiness, Pope John Paul II—March 2000)

So now You have apologized to everyone in the world
except my mother. Your mouth opened like cathedral doors
beneath the pure untouched steeple of your hat
and *I'm sorry*'s flung out like shiny coins being tossed
into the baskets of people's ears. Except my mother's.

Keep all those apologies—shine them up
and pray to them if you will.
I want 1979.   Rescind 1979. Give me back 1979
and your wide absence from my mother's needs,
your wide endorsement of her ignoble sorrow.
Give me back the seeds of ghosts sown in her eyes
when the priests told her to take it—
to take the absence of her own-taken husband,
to somehow—wrong as it was and a pity *tsk* a pity—
to take the fists that were mountains bad gods lived on—
take their arcs which traced a demon's wing on his right,
an angel's back on his left—take the bear hugs
and take them again, to take and to hold they said,
to pray for him and all the husbands who have gone astray.

I said give me back my mother's eyes
when your priests, all of them, told her she was married
before God and God was watching
and she must pray harder. And we did.
We did.

We prayed and made our hands campfires
hot with wishes pointed toward heaven,
pushed our palms together like pressing machines
that might press those wishes into prayers
beautiful enough for angels to pick up
and carry to our Lord—

I said rescind 1979,
when the entire world outside our house
was popping pills, creating little disco floors
with little lights flashing in everyone's suddenly pink brains,
everyone except my mother, sober as a burnt-down church,
kneeling at the kitchen table,
cracked tooth, hands letting go
of the repo notice, too afraid to see the doctor,
your priests her only last option. I said rescind it.
Rescind it all—the haematomas, the priests' cocksure
refutations that now stood between my weeping mother and
Jesus's wide embrace. Rescind it now. Rescind 1979
and I'll forget how she looked ornate in her misery and bruises
and how she picked up her Newports
and lit her last cigarette, nowhere to turn—
your churches nothing but walls
our personal tyrant could hide behind—

but you can't.
You can't rescind her last cigarette
and black eyes and empty pockets and good Catholic shame
for not being a better wife—the priests said to be a better wife—

nor can you rescind her two sons learning to cry without noise,
looking at her through a hole punched in the wall.
And you have no power to rescind the 3 white puffs of smoke
they saw rising from her, coronating a new secular holiness
in our vast and troubled land.

Burying Father

In Seaside Heights, NJ, my father would shade us
with his huge beer belly that curved down
over the copper snap of his red cut-offs.
My brother and I found refuge from the sun there,
beneath the frame that was a delight to bury.
He stood over us for the length of digging,
positioning so his shadow would shelter us.
The surface sand was easiest, ran through our hands
quicker than dimes as the ocean registered
the latest items of its ancient complaint. Then
the lower soil, compact, years of compression
(what did we know of compression?), harder
to get through, pull up, finally discard. We knew our father
wouldn't fit in any shallow ditch—too immense
for that easy burial—and so in the darkness we pushed.
Back then I hadn't read much but I had read about treasures
in *Boys' Life,* all sorts of value too deep for detectors,
covered by years of tidal shifts and wind's constant backhoe.
We never found anything. How I miss those days now—
in 25 years, my brother and I would be friends
who hardly speak, but in those days we'd shovel together,
doing our best to bury Dad. How we enjoyed his shadow—
a good darkness then—never thinking about the unhealthiness
of such an imposing frame, or anything as grave.

Another Poem on the Death of a Dog

The Greeks had the Oracle at Delphi—
a holy place where supplications were granted;
you had the refrigerator.
The sound of the cold cut drawer sliding open
equal in your world
to the Berlin Wall coming down in mine,
and you started your little funk dance,
as in your head, in some dog language,
the words were formed: *which meat?*
which meat? which meat? (or is it cheese?)
and your tail became your body's metronome—
a tail so beguiling I've seen you chase it
as if it were the chalice of Christ
and you a manic crusading knight.
So poor, you didn't even
have pockets.
And your stubby, flea-bitten
legs—how they kicked
when you slept.
Were you dreaming
that they were longer?
Or perhaps you were dancing
with a poodle somewhere in a dog bar
where they served dog drinks
and you could dip your snout
into the finger bowl of biscuits
the dogtender put out
to make all the customers thirstier?
In truth, you were a good dog, old friend,
purer in intention than any man.

What about all the murder? people might ask.
I tell them your tongue was democratic,
eager to accept all—from moth to woodchuck.
I tell the cosmos' jury that I saw you
let the cat go. That on this earth
you even shared the water bowl
with your greatest enemy.
I tell them how each whisker on your face
grew into a little divining rod.
I tell them all how your body was a duct
with pure instinct blowing through it,
a household-molded wilderness
that broke free once in a while,
went off into the woods unappeased
and, no matter how loud I cried for you,
could not be called back.

A Poem about a Refrigerator

(for Cat Doty)

A poem is a windy city, has broad shoulders
and insistent industry,
barrels into your brain, sticking
its steam-filled, swarmy head
into the delicate, empty bird cages
propped in the rooms of your imagination.

A poem can be rude, downright ignorant
of what you had been thinking about
and holding onto for too much of the day.
More than a city, a poem pushes its hemispheres
against your thoughts, knocking them out
of the windows of your ears.
Every good poem screams, "Read me
because you're going to die someday!"

I knew a poem that yelled, "Refrigerator!"
and my brain suddenly had room
for a refrigerator.
For me, it was all Goodbye
tax forms! Goodbye *I wonder if that check bounced!*

My brain was so full of refrigerator—
my mind full of that poem's world—
my whole head hard on the outside
and cool on the inside.

Upon Hearing That Baseball Is Boring
to America's Youth

(for Ed Romond)

And a tombstone sprouts in Wrigley Field—
    Send flowers to Fenway—
Put a black shroud
    over the house that Ruth built.

Let all the Little League fields
    across Kentucky and Los Angeles
shrivel to brown dead grass
    in the palms of summer—
holy cow, let's just turn 'em
    into golf courses.

The Mick is dead
    and Mel Allen's voice can't be heard
no matter how hard you tune a radio—
    the finesse of your fingertips
    rolling the dial to a frequency
    so thin
        your touch has to be as precise
        as Springtime's
            or Death's—

a finesse you learned on the left side of home plate,
    the ball bearing down
into that slice of percentages, that possibility of heaven
    that's your swing range—

and like a certain coincidence
    that occurs with practice,
you connect
    and the crack is like a starter gun
    and your legs start pumping
    before your brain thinks "run"
    and then your brain thinks "run"
    and your legs pump harder
    and there is the ball skating
    somewhere in your left eye
    and you stretch your hamstring
    to the white island of truth
    known as first base
    as the umpire sets up his court there
    and the ball pops into Jimmy's glove
    and you are barely safe
    in this impromptu pick-up game
    that saved you from an afternoon
    of nothing more than not being threatened.

Barely safe was what allowed freedom
in such sport—nothing ever guaranteed
and you had to know everything
going on seventy yards away—an outfield fly
was like a prayer and you were the team's
only angel to catch it. You were salvation.
It was about lining up; it was about advancing
the runner and you working to have a shotgun
arm; it was about no new equipment—
your glove like a pal that moves away
for the winter and returns with the cardinals,
blue jays, and blossoms for a reunion

in the spring. Indeed, each pop fly to you
your glove turned into a blossom, the ball
a bee-line from the sky into the sweet nectar
of out. It was about relying on an old pal.

The team was what mattered—
you did what you did for the greater society of 9
and you knew what you knew for yourself.
Boyhood existed within an outfield fence
and lines that clearly marked foul. Our bases
were knapsacks and library books.
Home plate was the Sunday paper—
we swung deep through the news above it.
Baseball wasn't boring; it was what saved us
from boredom. It was about how to swing
with two out and nobody on, how to field
with one out and a man on second. It was
fouling off the great pitches and cutting up
the good pitcher's one bad pitch.
The outfield was a big green waiting room
where we contemplated the virtues of patience
and spitting, equal parts of a gentleman's game.
We learned to read box scores and we learned to read
the sky, for the subtlest rain could wipe a day away.

It was about waking up
and looking outside and knowing
without a phone call that the other guys
were waking up and knowing without a phone call
to be on the field at 10—first 18 play first.
It was about feeling the sun on your back
as you watched from the outfield a whole world turning
around the bases, you a distant satellite
ready to relay any message that came.
It was about the game ending and everyone
going to somebody's house to watch Johnny Bench
and Pete Rose and Joe Morgan go up
against anybody else.
                  It was about Thurman Munson
closing his glove one last time
and that's how boys my age knew what Death was,
and we were able to talk with our grandfathers
about something large, tossing the ball across the wide chasm
the '60s created in everything else.
                  It was about imagining
Steve Carlton pitching Lou Gehrig. Cy Young
to Reggie Jackson. It was about playing
in those games ourselves.
                  It was about hope
in the face of school's fingernails
and winter's long breath. It was about
imagining hope.
                  It was above all
about trying to make it home.
You were an out-of-breath jeweler
cutting a diamond's edges
with your body. You were an amateur electrician
slapping together the circuitry of a run

that would juice the bleachers into noise.
You were a mere boy
who knew that tagging each base
was like gaining the knowledge you needed
to make it home. And when you dragged
your ankle across the plate's edge,
someone opened his arms
and yelled, "Safe! You're safe!"
and, for that one moment, you were.

Aubade

I love how this morning the world spills
around my breakfast plate, the newspaper opened beneath it—
Kosovo's rebuilding next to my toast
as my mug rests atop the list of celebrity birthdays.
Today's morning is large enough for Alfred Hitchcock and Don Ho
to have the same birthday, both residents now
on the continent of my kitchen table. The coffee machine
warbles its symphony of frogs and radiators
as if to sing of the arrival of the coffee itself.
The fried eggs start applauding.
Before I can stand, Victoria and her green eyes
float into the room and dock on the shores
of my table's new democracy, pouring me a cup.
And I want to be as precise with my joy today
as all those poets are with their suffering.
I want to tell you how on August 13th I was happy
even as the world surrounded my breakfast.
Now I see Fidel Castro and Danny Bonaduce share
this birthday also and they will forever be linked in my mind
with Hitchcock and Don Ho, and that's all right,
because this was the day the coffee and the light and
Victoria's sculptured neckline were pieces of my life breaking
open, and how they conspired to make the world
once more bearable again and again and again.

Bradford Gives a Lecture on the State of Modern Art to a Large, Distinguished Audience

Sometimes what matters is a good answer:
My friend Bradford, thinking Alvin Ailey,
Referred to them as the Alex Haley Dancers.

Some flurries of punches there's no stance for—
They're low and they're high and they're still flailing.
Sometimes a hard swift right is the only answer.

Laughter bloomed over Bradford like cancer—
Each guffaw, a punch, hurt him and ailed me.
He had slipped like an Alex Haley Dancer.

The audience was in a goddamned stir—
How does one count laughter? Does hurt tally?
Desperate and despondent, Bradford answered:

"I got what Hamlet sent Rosencrantz for—
Right here!" Then he undid his belt quickly,
yanked down, and bellowed, "Hail me—a dancer!"

Some escapes you must get down and prance for;
I know men born in the corners of failing.
When all that mattered was a good answer,
Bradford dropped his pants: the newest Alex Haley Dancer.

Upon Being Asked Why I Dedicated My First Book To My Mother When There's Not A Single Poem In There about Her

As Prometheus must have pocketed fire,
slipping it from Olympus in the folds
of his compassion and duplicity,
so my mother stole a *Webster's* pocket dictionary.
The Mansfield Jamesway Department Store
was all discounts and lighting that refused
to flatter, commerce sliding through its aisles
as my mother slipped that book into her jacket,
getting 30,000 words fatter. I know the arguments—
that's stealing; what about the owner?;
what about teaching her son what's right?
In truth, the entire Jamesway corporation
would go out of business twenty-one years later,
and I'm sure it had to do
with the *Webster's Riverside Pocket Dictionary*
whose pages held all the words of *Ulysses*
and *Paradise Lost* and *Look Homeward, Angel*,
but jumbled in alphabetical order.
What can I say? She stole a dictionary for me
because there were no words
a judge could use that would be worse
than her son starving
for a lexicon he could grip like a wrench
and loosen all those dumb bolts in his brain.

Receiving that dictionary taught me rectitude
and the many dictates that come down
from its cloistral mountaintop. I was suddenly rich,
a son from the most indigent family in Hampton.
How lucky—when I first started to rub against my language,
to sidle up to my own tongue,
my mother stole me a book.
Years later, I gave her one back.

Facetious

What uptight people say
when they want to
say "wise ass."
There it is—*facetious*—
all the vowels aligned
in alphabetical order—
the propriety of protocol.
O to say "Fuck off, wise ass,"
the vowels running backwards
off the wagging precipice
of the tongue, leaping ass-first,
floating every-which-way
on their willy-nilly parachutes.
The horrible, sad decorum
of the man who first came up
with "facetious"—how
he must have been repressing
a smirk as he said it,
tilting his head in the style
of Errol Flynn. A little more tilted,
his smile would run vertical—
a little wise-ass
on the face of facetious.

Pregnant

Like a frigate, she moves through the ice cream aisle,
docks at the frosted doors of the city she has been living in.
She reaches through the Breyers and Good Humor
and plucks out some flavor she's never had
but knows she'll love. Don't get in her way.
She is doubling in power. She is potential.
More than a ship, she has become a harbor—
this body of water that will break
onto our sure and otherwise dying earth.

Sex with Emily Dickinson

"I couldn't help myself," I told my wife.
"I was reading her before I went to sleep,
 and I can't control what I dream."
"What was it like?" she asked, wearily.
I started quoting "Wild Nights—Wild Nights,"
which she kept saying over and over—Emily, that is—
in the dream, but I didn't mention
the moment of climax
when suddenly Emily turned into Helen Vendler
and told me I was a bad poet.

My wife looked at me
 as if I had just burnt down a library.
"That's okay," she finally smirked, Zero
 at the Bone. "There's something I haven't told you.
The first time I read your book,
I dreamt I was in a threesome
 with Robert Bly and Robert Penn Warren.
We did it on a huge drum, men in suits
 banging in unison around us."
She paused.
"Maybe it was an Iron John thing,"
 then "I couldn't help myself."

We sat there awhile, nothing arriving
and nothing leaving, our dreams
causing a caesura of sorts. Finally I said,
"My sex, I'm sure, was more iambic than yours."
"You should know," she rejoined,
"I always hated sex that felt formal."

And we kissed right there, her lips
shaped like the light of a locomotive
at the dark end of a tunnel, which led to touching,
which felt like the rumbling of a waiting platform,
which led to great sex, which arrived
like one of those extra trains
they run on holidays.

After it was over we lay there
between the covers—words on opposite pages
in a book finally closed and touching,
which made us a sort of Braille upon each other
there in the dark, reading the language
that rose up from us all night.
A subcutaneous traffic had been loosed
and pulsed along the length of our bed.
As soon as we were Written, we were Read.

Mythology in the ShopRite

Not having a boat
or a whimsical chorus of Greek gods,
I am forced to live most of my Homeric epics
at the ShopRite in Washington, New Jersey.
And so it was a moment of moral significance
when my Wise Bravos Restaurant-Style Tortilla Chips
scanned at $1.50 instead of the sale price
of 99 cents. Their scanners hooked up to one great body,
like a Cerberus with 3 checkout aisles
guarding purchasing efficiency—
zip zip bag bag beep beep ch-ching
is the background muzak of the subtle hell I entered,
going to "Customer Service," armed with receipt and chips,
and recounted my woes.
                    Evelyn—Price check,
thundered down from the drop ceiling,
and Evelyn appeared.
Five minutes later, having checked,
she said, "No. It's a dollar fifty."
I said, "No!" and asked her to follow.
I was in charge now, armed with receipt and chips
and righteousness and the knowledge a tortuous journey provides.
We arrived at the aisle—I pretended I was Moses,
parting the wall of chips from the wall of soda,
leading Evelyn to the Promised Land, where everything
is priced accurately and Wise chips are only 99 cents.
"Oh, the 10 oz. are 99 cents—you have the 14 oz."
I said, "But then all the 14 oz.'s are behind the 99 cent sign!"
She said, "You should have looked."
"Are you unappeasable!?!" I screamed.

"Is the UPC code the new rock I must push up the hill?
The new eagle plucking at my liver?"
Her mouth parted like clouds:
"All right, I'll give you the 51 cents,
but don't tell anyone."
At the Customer Service counter it was counted—
two quarters and a penny, all of them glinting
like fire I had stolen from the gods
as I crossed the dark parking lot,
four extra ounces of Wise Bravos
than I had ever bargained for.

No Sex

"How long must I kneel before the altar?" I asked.

"Keep crossing yourself," the nun said,
"until you feel forgiven."

4 Metaphors. Nothing More.

There was one moment in my father's life
when he tried to hug me—

It may have been the unexpectedness of it all—
the usual handshake suddenly with dry gas added to its tank,
revving up into an embrace—
a collision of our bodies
after the wreckage of my childhood—

He approached—a bear
I had grown comfortable near
with a new, irresistible idea
in its bruin brain—
raising its paws toward me—

and I stood still
but must have shivered slightly away,
as if I were a city
trying to move
its locked-straight buildings
with all their hollow, echoing stairwells
away from an encroaching tidal wave.

The only thing wrong with these metaphors
is that the vehicles missed each other—
or that the bear stopped
because the prey was afraid—
or the tidal wave backed up
    because it somehow knew
    the city's infrastructure
    with all its strong facades
    wrapped around empty spaces
    could not sustain such a natural motion.

And there we were in the moment
    after that moment in his life—
a man and a man
    who happened to be a son and his father—
so close to hugging, standing there quietly,
    each second of silence constructing a monument
        to the only history we'd ever have—

We were each moths then,
        each the other's brilliance—
each of us unsure of soaring
    to the source of light we were so close to,
        not knowing whether we'd burn
            or finally be saved.

For the Children of the World Trade Center Victims

Nothing could have prepared you—

Note: Every poem I have ever written
      is not as important as this one.

Note: This poem says nothing important.

Clarification of last note:
      This poem cannot save 3,000 lives.

Note: This poem is attempting to pull your father
      out of the rubble, still living and glowing
      and enjoying football on Sunday.

Note: This poem is trying to reach your mother
      in her business skirt, and get her home
      to Ridgewood where she can change
      to her robe and sip Chamomile tea
      as she looks through the bay window at the old,
      untouched New York City skyline.

Note: This poem is aiming its guns at the sky
      to shoot down the terrorists and might
      hit God if He let this happen.

Note: This poem is trying to turn
        that blooming of orange and black
        of the impact into nothing
        more than a sudden tiger-lily
        whose petals your mother and father
        could use as parachutes, float down
        to the streets below, a million
        dandelion seeds drifting off
        to the untrafficked sky above them.

Note: This poem is still doing nothing.

Note: Somewhere in this poem there may be people alive,
        and I'm trying like mad to reach them.

Note: I need to get back to writing the poem to reach them
        instead of dwelling on these matters, but how
        can any of us get back to writing poems?

Note: The sound of this poem: the sound
        of a scream in 200 different languages
        that outshouts the sounds of sirens and
        airliners and glass shattering and
        concrete crumbling as steel is bending and
        the orchestral tympani of our American hearts
        when the second plane hit.

Note: The sound of a scream in 200 languages
      is the same sound.
      It is the sound of a scream.

Note: In New Jersey over the next four days,
      over thirty people asked me
      if I knew anyone in the catastrophe.

   Yes, I said.
   I knew every single one of them.

No Chaser

The appalling mercy of God—
a daughter is carried for seven and a half months
in the womb—long enough to incubate
the true love of her parents—
and her blood pressure drops.
C-section. The paltry child lives
for thirty seconds and dies
and is placed on her grieving, bleeding
mother's chest. Neither breathed for moments,
then the mother did. As for the kid,
they baptized and buried her.

Did I mention they're friends of mine,
these parents? From childhood, no less.
Why then do I keep
thinking of Richard Hugo slumping his shoulders
over the mahogany of the Milltown Union Bar?
And now I'm there with him, shooting back
Jack, stunned by the sudden fire on my tonsils,
and he turns and says, "No chaser."
But my throat's scorched by the whiskey
so I reach for the Rheingold
and he puts his hand squarely on my forearm
and says, "Nothing will ever burn you that bad."

Upon Learning That Hearts Can Become Stones

*In South Dakota, a dinosaur heart the size of a grapefruit is said
to have fossilized into reddish/brown stone.*

—*New York Times* (April 21, 2000)

And so scientists have discovered
what bartenders have always known—
given certain conditions and exposure
to harsh elements, even the grandest of hearts
can harden. In the Badlands of South Dakota,
they have discovered not only evident, larger old hearts
but that the smaller stones are hearts too.
We step over the most insignificant ones
all the time. We use rigid hearts to keep shut
doors that would otherwise swing open.
We form perimeters with them.
We imagine how a caveman used a hardened heart
to murder, bring down the blood muscle
of, say, a long-dead horse upon the skull
of someone who done somebody prehistorically wrong.
Scientists today are discovering small chambers
in the middles of cow fields and holding down
liens in law offices, half-hearts broken by prison
chain-gangs, and hearts from way out there
that burned in the night as they approached.
They have been busy identifying, scurrying to discover
the cause of why some hearts burn, others petrify,
but there is no science behind the various geologies
of the heart. So between the dried-up hearts
of fish and the dropping hearts of bats,
we walk toward our own deaths

with our own hearts, our mysteries locked
in these tiny strongboxes that somehow remain.
In the meantime we step on them, we break them,
we spread them on the drives that lead
to our houses. We print them on playing cards
and shuffle them with clubs and spades.
We grind the softest of them to chalk
so that our schoolchildren can learn our ways.

Trash

It was something like love
that called my mother up at 3 a.m.
to rise for the *Star-Ledger*—
deliver the papers to the paper deliverers,
her Chevy truck rumbling down Rt. 31,
passing the same cops, the same delivery trucks
heading northbound. It is something like love
that made that memory part of my history—
how many other moments do I have to pull hard on
to remember, like pulling a pike through
swamp water to eat it? Yet that comes so easily,
and now I can say it was love that put potatoes
and spam on the table. And it is love
that makes me cringe at the term "white trash"
because potatoes sometimes were all we could afford
and how we dressed is how we had to dress and I
watched tv a lot because everyone was working
or sleeping off the work and all the money we got
we paid to other white folks who weren't white trash
because they owned used car lots or worked
as loan officers and even though I am the only one
in the family who even went to college or graduate
school or is a professor and author and distinguished
fellow I am still a dopey student of this world
and love my family and how hard they worked and still work
but really worked then just to be called *white trash*
while giving me the wings of encouragement

and "day-old shelf" bread in my soup
to make it and write this poem which I write
because I love them and love them deeply,
old no-good-for-nothin' jagged-toothed white
white white trash that I motherfuckin' am.

Down to a Tune-Up

My father and I peer into the valley of engine—
all the hoses and pipes and hard reality
of combustion lying dormant
as we fiddle with what no longer works
well enough to get us somewhere.
We stand upon blocks but also swelling beneath us
as he ponders its power are my childhood
and his inability to even talk outside cracking
a good Irish joke. Like most bar joke-tellers,
he likes to be liked by a semi-anonymous audience.
But through all those silences and separations,
there was always this: a coming together
to fix an engine: a Fury, a Horizon, two Novas,
all tinkered with and somehow kept alive
for a few thousand more miles, a tire rotation
or two, several million contained explosions
deep in the wells. His father, a mechanic
with the same failure of silence
when a few words would do, more familiar
with the imprecise tools of his hands, not knowing
how precisely a tongue slices through silence.
I am here now, trying to get it all going, knowing
a few jokes myself, a few basics on how to keep
a dying thing running, working with my dad,
smiling with him under the hood, saying the words
that keep us going: *converter, viscosity, timing light,*
snug to a fit, pulling the plug and adjusting the gap.

Gravedigger's Requiem: Thanksgiving (2013)

At Thanksgiving dinner,
I am grateful for the scars
that have tightened into the letters
of a lifelong prayer
I say with my family,
then pass the stuffing and stuff what is past
into the corners around us.
The cranberry, please.
A slice of breast.
I am grateful.
Gone are the years of angry tides
roiling beneath our skins,
contention and disconnection,
monitions that yielded
the munitions in the hulls
below our tongues, the salvos
of a father's wrath, the return fire of the older son
who thought it was better to crack back on any attack.
Crack—   crazed—
it has all gone.

        •   •   •

Schiller said, "A tyrant's power has a limit."

        •   •   •

My father grew adroit
at squirreling himself away
in the darker corners of taverns
or just changing
bars completely—like a nut
we always had to guess
which shell he was under.

Often when we went looking for him,
it wasn't even pressing—
no tree had fallen through the roof,
the basement wasn't flooding,
no particular horror on the floor between—
It was the pedestrian,
gadfly terror that he
needed at least four hours of sleep
to make it through the night shift—

Our surmisals grew sharper with observing
his natural habit and habitat.
  Fridays—Harrington's Bar.
Mondays—Felix's Bar.
So it was Tuesday, Wednesday, & Thursday
that offered the most mystery—
three sisters we only knew
the last name of.

            •   •   •

Schiller said, "Brother, beyond the star-canopy
must a loving father dwell."

. . .

At Thanksgiving, Forgiveness has omitted
the hidden money. Absent
is the cracked knuckle of a cracked
man. Exculpation—thank you.
No longer are the brothers strangers,
and the necromantic pottage of rage and fear,
which once caused my entire bedroom to darken
and steam with its inexorable boil,
has been abrogated by Love
to a locked chest in a bolted closet
in a remote attic in all our unshakeable psyches,
the undiscussable keepsake, our family heir-
loom. Compurgation—thank you my friend.

. . .

Schiller said, "All sinners shall be forgiven / and hell shall be no more."

. . .

They were called bars
because that's what sprouted there:
Prisons grew all around the prisoners,
who snickered and wagered as they grew old.
The last call shout was their release hearing,

the overhead light was a door cracking ajar—
but they always committed the same offense,
and ended up right back.

       • • •

Schiller said, "Pleasure was granted even to the worm."

       • • •

And so, after half a life of looking
for him, here he is—
sitting in front of his son quietly,
twenty years sober—
After the cutting, serving spoons are used.

How exquisite is the meeting
of the eyes of the father
and the eyes of the son
who has forgiven him,
Forgiveness's three syllables the clicks of the tumblers
opening a safe's lock.
How extraordinary
that neither man says anything—
the quietness found on newly discovered planets—
neither one surprised
by how much is being said
by what's still.

       • • •

Schiller said, "The magic powers reunite what custom's sword has divided."
Schiller said, "Anger and revenge be forgotten / and deadly enemy be forgiven."
Schiller said, "This kiss for the whole world!"

·   ·   ·

At Thanksgiving, I am grateful for the noise
of Please pass the creamed onions,
and how they arrive through everyone's hands,
accepted then forsaken around our circle
as delicately as a tupperware full of pearls.
If I could, I would pass these onions down
to my great grandchildren
and instill in them the sense of
preciousness: These are the jewels
given by the king
after the dragon was slain. Quittance
is how we begin—

                thank you thank you.

·   ·   ·

Schiller said, "It is not flesh and blood
            but the heart which makes us fathers and sons."

·   ·   ·

I am grateful for how what sustains us arrives
after so simple a supplication. Please—pass—please.
I thank deeply whatever gleamed
in my old bedroom
that in my family, finally,
good wishes are what breaks a bone
and, today, grace begins everything again.

17 LOVE POEMS
WITH NO DESPAIR (1997)

How with this rage shall beauty hold a plea,
Whose action is no stronger than a flower?

—William Shakespeare

I

Not Rose Petals

Our love is not rose petals
or Valentine candy—
it is dirt and sand
    and the coarse pebbles in a shallow brook.

It is on our clothes, in our hair—
it is the foundation we walk on
and the soil we roll in
    all night long
    when we're away from each other.

It is not rinsed out by any rain
    or shower—
    we are so filthy with our love
that water will only run over it,
    not run it out.

Our love is dirt and sand
    and coarse pebbles in a shallow brook.

Whatever water hits us,
    our love makes it sing
      in its running.

Its song is the sound of this book.

II

This Is Right in Front of You

You better ignore this.
You better staple your eyes shut
and put pot-lids over your ears
and pinch your nose with vice grips
and cement your mouth shut
with real cement and while
you're at it or in it or whatever
cut off your hands for good measure

and when you are alone in your head
and the outside world is just a remote country
across a dark sea and your thoughts
line up in front of you, colorful rowboats
on the unsettled water, and when you see
the gigantic word they spell
is the same word you could never say
for fear its echoes would haunt you
out of your comfortable but shaky house—

when you see that you are in love
will you call my name then?

Yes, you better ignore this
or your life will collapse from beneath
you and you and your glass of iced tea
will have no map to direct you
to safety.

But if you don't ignore this
and are floating in the space between us
look at the stars overhead. Find the brightest
and pin any hope you have onto it.
Let your hope dribble in one long stream
back to the mountains of the earth.
And when the moon swings through this line,
lean toward that point. Form a long shadow
across our space and I will walk on it
as I always have—walking on your darkness
toward your still red lips where I will break
the cement, free the tools that have maintained
your careful face, expose your ears to the slight music
of the stars burning around us, open your eyes
and lift up your hands,

        then give your hands back to you.

Together we can become a library
of illegible knowledge, read the ancient scriptures
inscribed around the skin cells of our bellies,
the old writings that were born into our irises
which are as round as planets not yet walked on.
We can wall ourselves into our own dumb love
and together we will ignore everything. Everything.
No research will be done, just a deep reading,
unearthing a history that is happening now.

III

Her Hands Have Turned into Fists

What force they contain!
I try to open them
and find they resist
quite dutifully—
they've closed on the lines
gypsies have marked
her life with—
closed on the layer
of skin that grew yes-
terday, closed
closed on the echoes
they'd contain if I
whispered my loves
into her palms.
Those echoes would resound
quite beautifully
into the ears of the small
animals her bones have turned
into—large eyes and tiny
teeth, sharp enough
to see and chew what
almost isn't there.
Yes, I would like to
unclose them but she

just squeezes tighter,
the fingers whitening,
her skin receding,
the whole of her hands
becoming a ghost
around what she is
not holding.

IV

Losing Myself

I've tried diners and train stations.
    I've tried secluded mountains
and the bottoms of coffee mugs,

but nothing has matched the compacted loneliness
    inside me like the density of wind
dragging across the states between us.

As hard as the diamonds in your smile,
    the wind carries its hammers with no hands
and sustains a moan with no mouth,

seems to cradle solitude in its rough arms like firewood
    to be burned in my house as it passes through
and asks, "Where does she sparkle from?"

and tows behind it tumbleweeds and whirlwinds
    spinning with possibilities—"Perhaps there is a sea
inside her, perhaps untouched waters—

a pool that no one has swum.
    Maybe her shimmering eyes are evidence
of holiness in a godless world—

who else could have shellacked so perfectly?"
    This curious wind goes on,
"Or perhaps there is a darkness inside her

that is being shined into every time you talk.
    Have you ever been lost so deeply
in yourself

that no one could reach in to pull you out?
    You all have spaces, spaces
that you border with secret shores,

surround with moats of dark and cavernous oceans.
    You could distance yourselves with such darkness,
seclude the tender, sacred, and vulnerable landscapes

within you from the harsh alarms and pollution
    of a world that has lost its compassion—
make parts of yourselves dead like flowerwreaths

tossed off a ship that was too weighed down, lost
    until someone shines a wrist of light
across large plains and deep waters

onto what has been cast aside too long."
    And so I tell you, across this great land that is full
of empty spaces, I've been watching things spin,

listening to a sort of fury, losing myself,
    and finding half of us. I've been travelling
to prepare for this journey toward you.

Let me ride a jagged moon across your sky.
    Let me be a surfer of your dark currents.
Let all that darkness soak me

and let the light, the condensed light,
    guide me to a greater place. And get me there.
And then let me in.

V

Wonder Twin Powers Activate

The heroics I would pull if you were my partner—

You are form of a clear lake
           and I am form of a diving duck,
   diving into you, carrying some of you
   on my back, onto solid land.

You are form of an ice palace
           and I am form of blackbirds,
   flying through your closets,
   roosting in your crevices.

You are streams of the sky dripping through the rainforest
           and I am a baboon
   who can't get you out of my bristles.

You are a canal that knows a moon's pull
           and I am an escaped gator
   finding my way through your tunnels,
   arriving at a larger paradise that feels like a tide.

I want to be your wonder twin.
Whatever water you are, I am your animal.

VI

Instructions for Using the Tongue

Don't be too careful—
better to be effusive
with what the tongue can offer.
Sweet generosity returns to your soft mouth.

Be generous but don't be selfless.
We love the selfish tongue—the tongue
that believes itself to be important
moves easily over us.

When speaking, bang the tongue
off ceilings and into ears.
When licking,
             do the same.

You can build intricate traps
or whittle through walls,
turn a sucker to juice
and name a constellation.
Your tongue holds secrets on its surface, executes
spellbinding dances in the hall of your mouth.
Always pace. Never vent.
Your tongue is a precise instrument.

VII

"Making Love"

As if we could forge it,
    as if we had ovens
that could bake open
        whatever seeds
            are in us.

But could we sweat
    so wonder-
        fully profusely

without the notion
    of "making" something?

If we were to make something
    out of our bodies,
    why not love?
An end product
    we can only assemble
    with each other.
    We hammer, we shellack,
    and then massage each other's back.

We can make love with nothing—
    assemble it under bridges and on airplanes—
Let us create a masterpiece
    out of each other's skin—
It will be great art
    and how others would like to frame it.
Let us hang this piece
    in the long-hailed museums of our memories—
we'll be benefactors of a fleshy moment
    that could be admired during our many visits
        for years to come—
"the subtle craftsmanship!" "the mastery!"
    "entirely breathtaking!"

Even under the keenest criticism,
you will be able to hear that naysayer in you say,
    "Each stroke—pure genius."

VIII

Coffee

Honey, I hate mornings
    like a dead leg hates a polka.
I need a morning that brings back the word
      glorious,
reinvents it
    so that I can love breaking light again.

    I need you to wake me up—
    be the energy that fills my cup—
    Shake me awake with your wild inside
    till you see my day pop open wide—

    Let the sun shine over our backs
as we roll each other awake.
Let the skies change over us
and the sheets soil underneath—
    and there, my love,
    between the clouds and the dirt,
      let us find that morning,
    that elusive morning,
      where everything is glorious
      and the birds are references to the music
      coming from our bed.

I want you to be my coffee,
to pour down my throat,
make a Lazarus out of me.
Only you can take all darkness
right the hell out of me.

IX

A Poem for Men to Steal
& Read to Their Girlfriends

Whatever words are in me
aren't equal to the great granite walls
that house this bank inside me,
this great cache of feelings
that shine like laser eyes in a sensitive
security system. Here, my feelings for you
are a palm full of jewels and chokers,
garish and delicate. My other hand
a fistful of bank notes, pulled together as tight
as the tissue around my heart.

If only I could tell you—
if only I could steal some
out of this vault—a deposit box
so difficult to make a withdrawal from—
if only I could smuggle some of the gems
you have created in me,
carry them through the tunnel of my throat
into the sunlight between us
where they would glisten, I'm sure,
where we could examine them,
where you could see their worth
does not merely garner interest in me
but is rather what I have based all my checks
and balances on, what I look at in me

when I want to see what heroics, what savings
I should pull off with you. I appraise it every day—
it is what I value. See, I offer it here,
all my digits open to you, all the security guards watching
to see if your hand withdraws.

X

For One Who Almost Couldn't Admit It

Now that you've said you love me
have the willows outside your house
tossed themselves into a new frenzy?
For that little bit of opening,
have the ants crawled out of your walls
and piled their crumbs back into any holes
they came across, shutting you & your dwelling
up for good? Will there be no more irises
in your garden tomorrow morning,
or perhaps any rainbows that covet
your roof will melt into Rorschach pastels
in your gutters and birdsongs in your windows
turn into shrill shriekings as you recall
how, for one moment, you were as brave
and equal to beauty as that which you feel?

Can't a world end gloriously?

XI

Poem for My Friends

Tonight the old girlfriends are lingering
in the air, on the undersides of our eyelids, lining
up outside the doors we've closed
on the delicate toes of their needs.
All of us, each of us,
has found a love that's shut them out
for good. My friends, we've been drunk,
broke, beaten together. We've loved
each other as only men can.
So tell me, how did we ever get like this?

I saw it in your eyes, heard in your voices—the movement
of an ancient wind coursing across your smooth bones—
one by one you approached me—
"I'm in love," you each invariably said,
each unsure of what it meant.
I thought you were falling
from me, but now I understand.
I, too, hear those rainsticks,
those windchimes swaying with this strange weather,
that old rattlesnake with a slick flicker
wrapping up my jointed spine
and still rattling.

So let us toast each other and our old lovers—
the girls who let us undress them,
the girls who were patient with our fumbling,
the girls we no longer need
but refer to each time we learn.
May the roads that stretch before them
bend as easily as their curves
folded into our arms—the creases in us
still containing the lamp oil
we were lit beautifully by for a while.

XII

The Apple Orchard in October

Trees discover in their bodies
    a new brightness
their slow, dark wood
held like a secret.
The mountains bumper
this valley and contain
winks of wilderness that are purple
for today.
                    Tomorrow,
rainbows will float
from trees and turn
black, become soil,
and these hawks will die,
and we will die,
and everything will become soil,
and there is this moment
singing with color:

   Hurry!   *Hurry!*

and with these mountains nudging
us, you fly
into my widely opened arms.

XIII

Dating a Masseuse

Your hands are full of snap-
    dragons and wrap my bones in these soft bells.
From shoulders to butt to calves,

I lay myself out as you swaddle
    all my pain with evidence of softness,
with the fossils of ancient flowers in your fingerprints—

I feel a wind blows in you—you are full
    of wind and bend the stiff trees
toward a lake—

You are the moon pulling my tide
    into your forearms—
You are the warm shadow inside a fist—

If I were bread
    and if you ever kneaded me,
into your palms I would rise.

XIV

Under the Elm

We left the party, walked
beneath a moon that seemed
more a spotlight that night,
until we found a tree.
We pressed against it
and the grass rose around us,
the sky continued to darken,
and soon days, weeks, migrations,
and metamorphoses passed
as we kissed ourselves out
of our bored lives.

Us—two thousand miles away now,
the grass still growing wild
around our feet.

XV

Suzuki Dance

It starts in her body—
  a flame that makes her skin glow
like a lampshade around a belly full of lightning,
    spreads her light
   that is her
     into the world around her—

  yesterday she danced on a stage,
    today a creek,

       tomorrow—
    who knows tomorrow—
   but know she will dance.
There is no stopping this wild and precise woman
  who is moved only by instinct,
     unpolluted by thoughts
    of if and when and how and just
     is,
 with my eyes on her
   like oxygen to her flame—
  she loves a gazer's admiration,
    a net to capture the moment
     but release the energy—
 she moves quicker now,
    her feet thrust into the creek bed stones—
    a sundance in water,

movements of a dragon
                picking flowers—
the world, the sky, thoughts of love
   swinging around her,
   the great conductor's baton
                    keeping her time.

XVI

Enchanted, I'm Sure

You're no Cinderella and this is no glass slipper
I offer you—it is a book of poems
which you could probably see through
in severe sunlight like that prince's lucky shoe
(and this might even sparkle in places too)
but still, I remind myself, this is no fairytale—
our love is not rose petals or pixie dust—
it is dirt and wind-swept boulders and the faded clapboards
of the shabby green house you grew up in,
too small for your sisters and mother and you, and your father
long gone to Vegas and you hoping for some action
from that missing man in the purple snakeskin suit.
I have been to your old house and seen in closets
the lines of sequin dresses your sisters and you
used once or twice, a row of single shiny memories
full of dance and moons and bare shoulders. Tonight,
for the sake of romance, I'd like to swing
into your senior prom where you were stranded by your date
for some Wild Turkey in the parking lot, pick you
out of the crowd of hairdos, Soft Musk, and corsages, and spin magic
with you until midnight. No Prince Charming here, you know that—
I'd be your dirty little Elvis and you'd be my Priscilla,
Jailhouse Rocking out of the prisons of childhood pain
and abandonment—transforming that dark cavern of a gym
into a kind of Graceland—you'd dance close with the King
and all subjects we ever knew would bow down to this moment.
Our love, we'd know, is older than stars,

older than fibs and royalty could allow for,
and even the mice beneath the tight floorboards
would be happy that night. And when midnight calls, as it must,
and you and I recede back into rags and sorrow,
I would start my search for you, carrying into the world
what you've left in me—these poems, the thought of this book—
bringing it into villages and mountains and overgrown forests,
shaking up every fuzzy tree and shaking down every barfly
until I came across you, leaning against a screen door somewhere,
shucking pecans and drinking pop—I'd love every inch
of this path to you, from fading dreams to your feet,
kneel down, and know your real name, no fairytale,
know we were written by a great hand long ago,
and know how this book fits only you.

XVII

Words, Love Poems

Words, love poems, bah!—as if the loose-stitched tapestries
    I weave on these pages
could contain the intense light and honed edges
    found in the way I love you.

Tonight, my singular, I find banging words into this page
    to be too like hammering nickels
        into wooden beams—
too imprecise, not sharp enough
    to slip through the stacked tightness
        of aged grains—

how I've felt my feelings slip
    between this book's words
like warm breath through cold fingers—

Tonight, my soon-to-be-distant one,
    I would give you motions, not words—
the precise motion of, say,

ice melting off a shed's tin roof,
    forming pools of its changed, clear self
    in the midst of this sudden heat—

and if that pool grows to a frozen ocean in the frost of distance,
  then an ice cutter's hull, clipping its way
  through a frozen history,
  shattering the cool surface of your eyes—
  ice that could support the weight of my entire body.
  My boat would float through,
  making a path for whatever will follow in you.

Of pens, Shakespeare's, full of laughter and death,
  with a big feather at the end—
Or better yet, Neruda's—
  although I only speak English,
  when talking about love I prefer
  to feel my way through the rhythms
  of a language I cannot comprehend.

Of flames, passion.

Of skies, the sky at any time—
  how it is always full of greased movement
  and glides over this land.
  I would circle around your skin
  and continue indefinitely
  the way weather loves a planet.

Of pottery, a vase in the kiln's desert—
  the movement is in the hardening
  into something beautiful, the evolving
  in this great heat into something that can hold
  whatever will be passed between us—
  my movement would continue beyond our lifetimes.

Of storms, a long, soft drizzle,
    knocking over nothing
    but softening everything.

Of animals, the book worm
        boring my way through shelves of love poetry,
        still hungry, until I hit the space for this book
        which is not there
        because it has been given to you.

I know these words are not sustenance enough,
        cannot content the appetite we create
            in each other,
        but know my body is moving
            behind each word—

the way you move me
as my pen reaches the end of this book
is always toward you.
See? You are holding the trail I've left.

LANDING IN NEW JERSEY
WITH SOFT HANDS (1994)

Introduction

Idaho trails from my left penny loafer,
Arizona from my right.
A Nevada waitress hangs from my heart.
The many loves of the many states
are crushed into my wash-needing socks.
My ears still cling to the musicians
I've loved in these places.
There is here, in my pocket,
a memento for you.
It is a sound,
and if you could open it,
your very palms would shiver
with what my travels play
in the small, well-boned ears
you have in your hips,
      your legs, your ankles, your feet.

Are you dancing?

Hometown: Alliance, New Jersey

On the fading streets of my Alliance
the girls with soccer balls cross puddles
in their own little rivers of desperation—
each one a teenager, each one inheriting
the teen-age world. The mechanics who watch
with eyes as big as their mouths close the hoods
on cars as they have closed the hoods
on their women, working on them as needed.
Everything is beating, beating, beating
in this town. The sun has become relentless
in its insistence to pin us. The wildflower garden
is overtaking the grammar school.
And the bed above the tavern cracked
the floorboards when another man clenched up
into a huge sexual fist with MiMi—
Alliance's first hooker. She's so good
even the German cop likes her. Right now
a man hands her ten dollars and she
kneels in front of him, changing yet another thing.
But what has changed here? The brant geese
still return in May, the borders of the river banks
still break down every hard rainfall. Dinner is being cooked,
the cooper is closing shop, and in the barnyard
a chicken discovers a worm it finds delicious.

The First Thing to Say

At Port Colden Grammar School
we were filed down
the steps into cement halls
when the blasting of bells
crashed through on playtime—
how one drawn out bell meant Fire
and Fire meant fresh air
while three quick punches meant Air Raid.
This is how we learned the rhythm of bells,
crouching in half-light with our books
over our heads, hoping that hard knowledge
could stop bricks and cinders.
And with the bells intruding on us
like the aircraft closing in above,
everyone was laughing at Jimmy Muzecki
who could make people laugh at anything,
even things that weren't funny.
As I crouched I tried to think
of the first thing to say
in this commotion, how this could be it—
no more milk shakes or turtle-hunting,
no more dodgeball, no pez,
no Christmas—the big IT
and we're just down here giggling.
Now Carey Kresgie was punching Farting Charley
and Charley was farting.
Everyone was happy with this.

The first thing to say, I thought,
would have to do with the stupid,
the clanging overhead—cacophony
in a space where air should not be raided,
where safety had to do with depth and books.
I would tell them, I would tell them
all. But Jake and Nate were standing
and sitting, sometimes flailing
their arms—daring to be picked off
by Miss Skunkmuffin—and everyone was dying
with laughter.
             So the first thing to say
would have to be silly, I thought,
something for whoever would listen,
tired of bells, wanting to hear something
that had nothing to do with the crumbs of cement
that would drop about us.
                        Above me,
I could hear the engines approaching, unstoppable
as the locusts; I imagined the bomb doors
opening, spilling their shiny, jewel-like cargo
onto the courts and markets and schools below,
onto Mr. Johnson sweeping his splintered stoop,
onto Mrs. Wimfleson and her hairless poodle "Smooches,"
onto my mother, onto Carey Kresgie's mother,
onto all our mothers and fathers and sons and daughters—
unloading their godawful yawns and guffaws
to shake the words right out of my mouth.

On the Last Day of the End of the World

The rock is what he knew—
he knew the hard weight of rock.
This went on for years—
the slow, uneasy rolling of weightedness
      followed by an unwinding, what else?
And for years he studied it—
how everything pushed will eventually push back—
and he knew nothing of breaking,
    of suddenly not pushing
        or not being pushed,
and so he decided nothing.
To him there was hill.
And there was rock.
He used to think that rock was his burden,
but now he knew it was hill.
He was tired of pushing,
    yes, and of being pushed,
and he knew the rock wasn't tired
    of being rock,
nor the hill tired of sloping.
By now he had forgotten
why he pushed the rock
so when someone yelled to him,
"Why do you push? It will only push back
    and the world is ending,"
he, who knew nothing of ending,
    looked up and said,
        "Leave me alone."

And so the people left the myth—
buildings fell, the ground split,
and the planet rolled across the surface
of the sun, becoming part of that new fire,
losing its old sensibilities, and, against
the efforts of all that had been there, ended.

Shakespeare as a Waiter

He was tired of the old ladies
    wanting cappuccino, of the little kids
with their chocolate milk or two cherries
    on a plastic dagger—anything to consume
his time while he had more important things
    to do—a fair lady in booth three was dying
for a reuben, and twelve lit professors
    wanted another round of ale and song in the lounge,
and his entire tip probably depended on it.
    This is where he started to learn timing—
when to allow the waiting, when to deliver
    what will last a while.
His boss started yelling—"Shakespeare!
    Bus your tables!" He was tired of this too.
He was tired of picking up and wiping down,
    tired of people's half-eaten burgers, tired
of Caesar dressing, of angry leers, of all the spit,
    tired of the cooks who called him "Willy,"
tired of directing people to the bathroom
    when he had so much more
direction to offer.
        But he didn't reject this—
    none of it. Instead, he took it in,
studied it until he understood it.

In his mind, things grew large—
    first nothing, then nothing
became an ocean
    dotted with islands—
each island had a name—
    Venice, love, Denmark—

    a dark count started to form,
witches sang,
       stars crossed,

and Shakespeare,
       between the napkins and ketchup,
    lit a table's candle
and waited for the evening shift.

Flightless Bird

I know I don't hold road
as sacred as hawk must hold
air, but driving through Bald Eagle
State Forest I must have glimpsed
a little of that wind religion.

                    •

Warblers strum the instruments of their bodies
in rivergrass fresh with snake musk.
They are belting,

                    all of them belting,
We are here!
        We are here!
                Yes this is where we are!

                    •

This is what I want to be—
an extension of something here,
something now—that sweet something
that won't grasp you or be grasped—
that dark, sugary, evolving something.
It's that air, that road
between my ribs.

                    •

I know the exact size of my bones
the way hawk knows angle,
circumference, the perfect art
of circle. It's the inherent knowledge,
the only religion we can believe in
by praying solely within the cathedrals
of our own bodies.

．

                              And who,
after seeing the flowing
and dipping, gliding
and gyring, can argue that hawk
is not an extension of air?

．

The spruce rise like nine thousand steeples
and if I could stop this car on this road
that never seems to end
I would kneel before this blue altar of sky.

Yes, this is where I am,
the religion I know for now.
It is found in the personal,
the slow revelations that have always
        been true for me,
the ones I'm just coming to
            now
        in this state forest.

And here, in the cracked angling
        of pines,

a wind stirs up inside me.

·

Drunk Again, I Stumble Home on Euclid
and Cut Across Thornden Park Baseball Field

I.

Tonight the trees bend over like broken
old women picking up their husbands'
empty whiskey bottles.
The film of sky never
runs out of frames, never
runs out of dynamism & greased movement—
it moves quicker than my blood.
Doesn't it always come to this?—an awareness
dancing with my great ignorance. How right now
underfoot
the moles are squealing,
dying, making love, sliding through the dirt
that holds me up, holds these trees up,
holds itself back, compact,
and how goddamn strong the sky is—
how sky holds up planets
like polished marbles shot into dark grass.

A barn owl slides down from the sky
onto a mouse—just like that.
I round third
and head for home.

II.

Tomorrow I will wake to vacancies
I know every inch of,
a camera full of negatives;
dead whiskey will swirl inside me
like a warm rain stirs the sky
before sky flashes down onto pavement,
soaks the mailman, pours over
growling dogs, drenches car dealers,
and affects everything that walks through
with its perfect wetness.

Bleeding Jesus

Sitting in catechism, the priest punching Jesus
    into our heads, I stared into the dank hallway
beside the room. My attention snapped

to my hands, rapped by Father Longinus's ruler.
    He talked about the cross, the thorns,
the slow driving of nails. It was the pain

that interested my nine-year-old mind,
    the coincidental pain of our hands—
hard, deliberate. I ran home

and told my mother that I was Jesus, the Son of God.
    She slapped me twice and banished me
to my room, which only convinced me I was Christ.

The next day, I told some classmates
    I was Jesus. They didn't believe me
until I named them my apostles—

Saint Hank, Saint Milo, Saint Fat Eddie.
    I was ready now for the pain, the crucifixion.
We met at Happy's Ice Cream Parlor for a last supper—

the cone was my body, chocolate fudge my blood.
    Fat Eddie had seconds.
We couldn't find a good cross,

so they tied me to a swingset in the schoolyard.
    I told them to leave me but not forsake me.
They acted sad, as was planned, and left.

As the night gathered itself, I started
    feeling lonely, hungry. My arms tired
from the spread I was in—the opening of an embrace

that was never able to close, to enwrap.
    How prone a god can be.
I noticed a patch of wild blossoms

at my feet. They were small, purple.
    They looked easy to kick up, so open
and convenient—their thin, sweet petal-meat

would be a wafer on my tongue. And I thought
    of why I was there, how it was no fun
being Jesus anymore. I left the blossoms

where they were, as I had found them, and screamed
    for my father to come get me, to untie me,
for it to be finished.

Something You Haven't Found

The world is okay, Karen,
so put down the gun.
When all the right things are too soft
and the worse things are hard—
when you touch your life
and it gives too easily,
like an eaten-out peach
that should be thrown from the barrel—
when you're a fire waiting to blaze
but can't find the kindling—
the world is okay.
Even when the tight muscle of sky
relaxes
and hail hails all over—
who could have guessed there's so much
hardness in the air?—
the world is still okay.

.   .

It is the softness you want.
In fields, you revel
in the chicken hawk's wide circles—
you say they encompass your heart—
but you turn away from the fantastic descent
upon a bluebird, much preferring
the easier part of nature—
say, the slow, slow bulbing of tangerines
on a low branch, or the kiss of water
upon a river oak's root.

• •

We come from the water
and what could be softer?
The stream behind my house
divides at the bed of sand
and rain will lay its weight
in the slightest of my lawn's small valleys.
Water will pull through the tiniest cracks
of anything you own
and tongue them clean.
And still it can drag canyons out of solid plains
and put out fire.
Yes—the soft can wear away the hard,
so put down the gun.

• •

Sometimes we get caught up
in the hardness—it nets us,
scratches our lives. My uncle
chose death in an inn after my aunt
had left him. The bartender said
he sat down, seemingly sure of everything
he wanted, and ordered a shot of Sambuca—
the sweetest shot in the house.
While the bartender poured it, my uncle
pulled out his army pistol
and blew that flame into his own dampness.
Death must be hard, Karen—
it can scatter anything—
and that's why I choose life.

It's full of softness—
it flows into valleys
and leans toward the moon.
How it steals up at an intimate moment
between lovers,
and can go away as quick and jarringly
as a newborn calf's neck
can snap.

.   .

And so when death becomes a soft word
in your too-perfect ear,
when you lift it up
and put its nozzle in your mouth,
when you think it can make you blaze,
when the void seems just an extension of your house—
know right down to your fingertips
at the end of that trigger
lies nothing you can hope will be
better, softer, more reassuring
than life. All I can tell you, Karen,
is that the world is okay.
The world is okay.
When secrets slip out,
secrets you didn't even know about—
when surprise and vulnerability
kiss on your doorstep
and desperation frequents your windows,
pull them to you. Squeeze them
into your chest and know
the softness it takes not to be hard.
When you have eaten everything

you can think to eat—
when your cupboards are empty
and your garbage is full
and you're still hungry
for something you haven't found—
put down the gun.
When the world is a tidal wave
nearing your block and your house
doesn't seem as sound as it once did—
put down the gun.
A sycamore bent with hard wind
will still bend back
and will embrace that wind
with all its leafiness,
let itself be pulled,
feel the slash and tug
of its own weight,
and will still bend back
when hard wind turns soft.

．

Anima

She leads me into an empty bar
where the jukebox records haven't changed
for years, where we could slow dance
on a stool and, when she's drunk enough,
she could tell me how she needs to love me.
What does she want?—she wants what every woman
in my life wants—for me to stop being such a jerk,
and I know this. I tease her with my maleness
just to keep her on her toes. Tonight
we've got a date—we're meeting for dinner,
where we'll negotiate once again our separate needs,
trade secrets, decide how to walk perfectly, no tripping,
almost a ballet of silent touchings and consequence.
I'm bringing the wine, she's bringing everything
she knows I'll be lacking.

Inspiration

It crosses me three

times and wraps me like

Jesus in words and the

places between words, the

inspired, breathed-in

places that are found

in all of us, the spirit

of lightning—it connects us

like words, connects the

words like something connects

us—creation, creation.

Love on the Assembly Line

The assembly line would keep going,
    even when he fell behind
production.
        As he filled the boxes he knew
            he was full of her.

But the warehouse was no place
                for love,
    and that made him a rebel
for bringing love in.

    The workers knew something was up—
he opened doors for them,
      he drank his coffee slow,
    he was always late on Thursdays.

When they approached him about it—
    when they had him
      and his love in a corner—
they wanted to know everything.
    And, because he was so full
of what they needed,
        he gladly gave it up.

The workers took it all,
    labeled it, put it on the line
to disassemble it, see how it ticked.
They lined up
    the length of the factory, and with this chain
      they held the love down,
took it apart one nut at a time,
        examined every screw.
Soon a piece of his love was in everybody's hands
    and their hands started to hum
      with his broken down heart.

They never gave it back to him—
      instead they took their pieces of love,
    placed it in other things—
    cars, stereos, generators—
some ate lunch
       with the love they'd never share,
    some brought it home
      and put it on a proud mantle,
and some voted for the President with their love.

And as far as he is concerned,
    he whose love is in the hands of others,
he trolls the evening streets
    looking for what may be discarded—
a leg, perhaps,
    that his love used to stand on,
    or maybe a battery.

The hand that held his love
          now collects time and calluses,
     and at the factory
everyone is happy again,
          everyone filling boxes,
          everyone pushing buttons,
everyone doing what is necessary
          to assemble the perfect working machine.

A Few Good Lies for the Personals

First the easy ones:
I wrote the great American poem.
I am a millionaire. I am so handsome
you will be afraid to touch me
but I am humble enough to let you.

But *too* easy—only something more subtle
can match my best badness.
If I were to lie, I would tell you
I would hurt you—that your heart
will never be broken
as roughly as in my hand,

and you might be intrigued.

I will tell you how I pray
    that your skin be my only redemption—
how I will spread over you
                        farther than the rivers—
with more energy than the world's only remaining
                undiscovered ocean—
to make you wet with my badness
and watch the sun swing over your body,

and I'll swing it over again.

Yes, I'll lay the blocks of my immorality so high
      that your fences will be in no position to bargain.
Then I'll let my stones crumble,
                        however you'd like;
let you see
        how low they can go—

how no threat, no psalm
   could ever bring a weight onto me
        as the truth of your fingertips can.

Saturday and She's Still Gone

The cup of black coffee sits on the morning newspaper
and it is mid-afternoon after a night of sleeplessness.
The clichés race around my mind like wild chihuahuas
running through a house they won't leave
and I can't kick them out: "Pick up the pieces,"
"Life goes on," "Fish in the sea"—
yeahyeahright. Sayitagain, sayitagain.
That doesn't explain how an absence
can be such a presence, how all night
that absence lay down with me, rolled over,
spread itself across my face and wouldn't
let me sleep until morning drooled
its ugly light all over me and another day.
Those clichés burn the toast with me
and curse the cat with me right out
the catdoor into the world of rain and fuckheads,
but they don't say how loneliness has piled up
and is spilling over the sugarbowl
as I reach for a spoonful of sweetness.
Those clichés walk down Broad with me
but don't account for the gall in my chest
pockets, the bitterness I pull out and rub my head with
as I pass two lovers here, two there, on a bench,
a bus, a corner, a parking lot, a newsstand,
another corner, near a mailbox, a plugged gutter,
plugged against the rain and sun
and greasy pollution Syracuse spits up
to that great Nothing of sky all morning
and evening and day as I walk
with my eyes open but mouth closed—

no reason to open this mouth—
none at all—no lips to touch,
no kind words to put out—I'll just shut up now
(yeahyeahright, sayitagain, sayitagain),
open to page two—maybe fold the wash
in a little bit, maybe call her
"bitch" or "baby" or something
a little more truthful, maybe do nothing.

Delaware Water Gap, NJ Side, Election Year, Rush Hour, Hungry Again

The sun slips like a tongue
    down the sky's neck
and the flowers within me

open to it all.
    The world has lost its money
so I have wandered into these crags,

tall pitch pine, ascended
    the shins and thighs
of this state to escape the bars

where drunken laughter is overcome easily
    by the things of this sober world,
where the television's wide embrace

pulls us into lay-offs and mortgages.
    The entire arm
of the Delaware reaches for an ocean

as the cars of our lives reach for something
    we each call home.
Right now in Hampton, my floor is filled

with lottery tickets, sweepstakes
    forms, fast money that is always
six numbers away. I've left that for now

to be part of this larger body. There is something urging
    about the silhouettes of silos
standing in the setting sun. I will be part

of this mountain—I will budge
    only when the entire skin of this cliff
budges—avalanche or the subtle rubbings

of erosion. I will do well to make
    like this cliff—that egg—
a tree, a cloud—where what is larger

sings in accordance
    with our smaller concerns,
where the gap is what we cannot believe,

where sky can offer a constance
    of nothing,
and where the bushes

won't grow fatter each year,
    their dumb, prone, and delicate lungs
full of this less rich air.

Monopoly

There's something sad about the steam
pouring out the tenement vent.
Puerto Rican lovers double down
the steps into the concrete dusk.
Baked negroes look for shirts
and children stare at squirrels,
amazed at the mundane.
Broken windows are like black eyes,
wine bottles drop like dreams.
Fire hydrants stand forever—
statues of heroes that never were.
Between walls,
wet sheets are hung to dry—
at night they can't be seen
through the fog.

On the other side of the night,
some guy doubles down
and loses a hundred on
the turn of a card.
Close your eyes—
fat men belch like frogs
at the shore of a pond
filmed with flies.

This Is Just to Slay

(a song of 1992)

I raised your taxes exorbitantly
and then cut them
after you were starving.

    Forgive me—
    the steak I bought with my senator's salary
        was so hot and juicy,
    and the wind that blows through the capitol
        is so cold.

In Defense of Syracuse's Loose-Knitted Sky

When the heat drops from the sun and needs no gravity to land
    hard and bounces off the hood of your old Volvo the way holy
    thoughts are rejected by the hard shell of science—

When prairie fire swings its hot arms into your fields and sings its
    falsetto into your sky and your house, your dog, your cigars
    and your lemonade just stand there in the path of heat's
    widening circle—

When heat crouches low, a heavy, pregnant beast full of
    destruction, and crawls up the road, softening the hardest
    blacktop, scorching the sideweeds, scratching stretch marks
    behind its wide berth,

slithers up your body and spills down your throat
    like a 90 proof shot of yesterday's thirst—

When heat does this, get your ass to Syracuse.
Go to Syracuse in February, say, when no one is thirsty, when heat
    is just an enigma like the promised word of God to the Zionists.

Stay there.
And when it snows, when the skies have carried the Great Lakes to
  you and dropped them like the Earth's soiled white laundry all
  over your front lawn and pet shih tzu—Syracuse's prank on
  all its people—

Think about Rt. 44 in South Dakota, how heat's ugly dogs will
  run into your car, pop your radiator, blow into your engine,
  and leak their dry cracks all over your leather interior.

And when sky falls down in April thirty drops at a time all over
  your freshly washed bicycle, think about the lopsided sky over
  Phoenix, all sun and glare and spilling sunburns,
  no rain,   no water,

            no water—

Heat can bake your pie,
but it can't build your filling.
It can rub your neck raw
but it can't kiss your body—
what kind of lover is that?
Let rain be your lover.
Let the many mouths of the sky
drop onto and suckle your body
in your body's many small places.

Let the rain lick you out of the bad mood
you bought in L.A. and can't exchange.
Let it fill you past your full mark.
Let the rain form waterfalls where your body needs to laugh,
and let the waterfalls sprout up like orgasms on a good night.
Let yourself be so full of the sky's good humor
that even the snow, happy and awkward
in its own many bodies, is no surprise—
how the rain, put against the dryest,
most miserable of land and thoughts,
can cause tulips, turnips, potatoes, and rainbows—
great colors bordering our rooves, crossing our town.
Let the rain water your spirit and let your spirit
continue to rain on others.
Indeed, let our spirits open as wide as our umbrellas—
how umbrellas are both male and female,
like any blooming flower.
Joy to the world. It is raining.
And the moments of our lives run deepest,
like our favorite valleys,
where they are most moist.

Dissatisfaction with Great Expanse

(a cry for long-distance lovers)

To know that our bodies are on the same highway
      but two time zones apart
does me no good.

    Distance has placed a roadblock
      on the freeway—
a lump in our mashed potatoes.

The highways of America don't interest me—
    I'm much more interested
in the freeways of your body—
    the turnpike that runs down the front of your neck,
over your clavicle,
    between your untouched breasts
    where I'd gladly make a pit stop,
along the ridge of your stomach,
    and will take me—

    I've been there before—

    into your great continental divide.

That is when I will be connected
　　　by highways with you—
　　　how our roads will converge,

　　　　　　　　　　　　　not fork,
　　　where the hard asphalt softens with the day's heat
　　　and the toll taker puts his hand out
　　　　　　expecting the kind of money

　　　you gladly waste in exotic nations.

Some Kind of Storm

Last night a hurricane blew into Lafayette, Lafayette
    where Sara and I once lay
with the wet angels in the tall grass
      on the banks of Rt. 10.

All of Louisiana shivered at midnight
    when the storm hugged its banks,
      questioned its borders,
blew all sensibility and orientation
    to a place known only by the damned and certain dogs,

and the City of New Orleans shook
    with a new kind of music.
The houses started to dance, a rumba
    with dips
                followed by a stillness
    New Orleans didn't know.
And it was just another dance to that city of fedoras and pregnant women.

But in Lafayette, Lafayette
    dropped its accent for a wind
as cajun spices blew up into small whirls—
    curry in the sky
      came raining over the highways
and drivers cried all the way home.

And all I could think of was
Sara's mouth, how lost I became in her pocket of moans,
     how that night a storm stirred up in my chest, my legs,
my arms, as I lifted her and her own storm
into the soft grass, below the headlights
     and noise of the passionless.
How our storms diverged, drenched everything,
and how all this was finally equaled in Lafayette

by Andrew, Prince of Motion,
     as he shoved into walls,
                    broke through rooves,
driving everything,
                    relentless,
     to get to the heart of the city,
to throw some spices in the air like a dangerous confetti
     only lovers and certain dogs could appreciate;

and how Andrew, when Andrew left, took
     Lafayette with him, and dissipated only with distance
and the promised fading memory
     as generations grow older, forget,
fall out of love,
          build houses they'd improve on,
     and settle for them.

A Note to Karen

It's in our hands, our
voices, the spontaneous moments
we wait for, build with.
It may be as small as a sweep
of hair on a nonexpectant arm, or
as large as your glance into mine.
It is in the small moves and pauses,
and the movements in the pauses.
It is the whittling, the allowed
carving, the shaping
to allow slips, the molded hollows
in us worn from containing
and releasing, holding and letting be.

The Dying of the Light

The pine barrens 50 miles south of us
kill themselves every ninety years.
The way they live—hoarding sunlight
and rain—pirating away the lesser
parts of the woods until only the fewer giants
remain, making a thinner forest.
And Father, you've done it now.
You've smoked and drank and smoked
and drank your way right into the body
you're dying in—the body that frames you
but no longer supports you. It's broken—
it's breaking you. It's full of shadows
and caves where it should be solid and overgrown
with a body's own full-rooted days.
Empty, empty—a bloated, empty shell, full
of echoes that ring "empty, empty," full
of echoes whispering woods' crooked intent.
Like the pine barrens. Yes, the pine barrens.
When winter drags its callused ass down
the bark, its fingers of ice scratching their way
behind, brittle needles fall to earth and wait
for that one leg of electric sky to tromp their thirsty bodies.
And then the flames. And then there's more
flames. And you still smoke now,
lying in this hospital room. In light
of all this, what can be said? The walls
are cleaner than your insides. You know
it's getting late. Pill to sleep. Needle to live.

Father, in every woods there runs an evil,
a Jimmy Leeds* who'll stir up the ground
with whispers that become echoes in later years.
And then this: one is left lying in one's rotting,
incinerable forest. And below one's back,
every needle has a horrible secret.

---

* Jimmy Leeds—the name of "The Jersey Devil," a creature in pine barrens folklore.

To Grandmother, after a Photograph of Joseph Cornell

Man is no longer water to me; he is
light: the soft light of a bird's belly

or the slow filter of lace curtains. He
is found in windows and mirrors, weakens

in corners and the tint of memory.
                         Whatever light
you were, you had,   whatever—

it's gone. There was water at the wake,
tears over your shell, but—I will not lie—

there was light. Hard, undulating light—
the insincerity of relations, the cold light

reflected from dead flesh.
                      And I know
the danger of being light in light, drowning

in it like water. I go to the dark sea,
stand on a crag, wait. The balance is here—

the undetectable places where rock ends
and sea begins, where sea and sky lick,

where the moon drools thick
on passing clouds, and the stars spear everything

and nothing. I stared into your eyes,
two flashing seagulls. Here, gone.

It is the dimness I fear.

Yellowstone

The lake is a riddle—
it asks itself over and over again.
To know the answer, you must own water—
even the water of your own body
would suffice. The lake beckons to be heard
as only the lonely can hear it—
a radio signal with a very specific destination.
It throws itself onto the shore
at your feet—are you lonely enough
to answer it yet? The answer lies
in how well you throw yourself
into the water. There are answers
in the depths—loves to be reckoned with.
Look again at the flat promise
of so much water—how it will swallow
you, all of you, like rain.
This lake is a riddle—
it asks itself over and over again.

Movement

It is noon and the farmer is dying.

The sun presses the barn's broad chest

and hot chickens breathe. The wheatfields

breathe. A haziness falls every-

where—it fills the wheelbarrow, mats

down horsetails, rubs against the stones.

Mud cracks and sleeps, cracks again. The barn door

wheezes open. In the hayloft, wet kittens squint.

Life in the Blue Danube

san francisco, July 1992

The sidewalk stretches into its own
cat-like tendencies, and the waitress
knocks over a chair.
                    There is my world,
the beginning of it—
                    if Kevin were here,
there might be a yellow-tinted drunk
slumped against a parked Subaru,
or something he'd wish to invent
but not let himself.

                    There—Kevin is now
a part of our world, reader,
and now so are you.
                    If I could,
I would let this poem call out
to every corner of our puny sky
and pull in ornate onks, boomerangs,
slow-moving glaciers.
                    If I could
this poem would stretch out, too,
and on it we could walk
right into the next page,
        where possibilities stick to your smile, run through your teeth
        just as bag ladies pirouette through Indiana cornfields.
Invent. If you already know it,
there's no reason to write it.

The Artist in New Orleans: Storm Showers Rain Wet

The egret on the state line
    craned its neck to the soggy sky
and saw, maybe, what was to be
    a spectacular sunset
            if not for the hurricane—
    the sky was something like a seed
        from which light could eventually grow,
    could fall
        over the fields, over the beans,
over the cows slowly rising
    to move to their feed,
also wet now, as is the scarecrow,
    the land itself, the many bridges
people make everyday,
    to travel over what the rain
        has made before—

Bourbon Street was growing louder with our own nature,
    and soon the sky
        and all it held
would tickle the city's pavement,
                would dance
over the egret, around its strained neck,
    and over the many seeds
      the egret is looking over—
    each seed a whisper
      of more rain to come,
    of wet possibilities, of sproutings,
      of more poems to be,

more words to be born
with pursed lips
and swinging hips,
words that carried umbrellas
but forsook them
just to dance with the freedom
empty bottles are filled with
when a storm shakes them into a music
they never contained
or rattled
before.

The Fury

In high school, boys who aren't bad do bad things
    just to not be good.
This is the way it was that day we rebelled
    against the cafeteria,
much preferring the Burger King, two towns away.
    I had just bought my first car,
a 1970 Plymouth Fury, and, although it was tested,
    I wanted to test it. Mr. Burns, who it was rumored
didn't have any hair on his balls, walked the parking lot
    like Cerberus during lunch, waiting, watching
for bad people, trying to keep them in school
    near the good kids. We didn't care,
and once we made it to the Fury my key broke
    into her ignition as if it were the first time,
and when I turned it she hummed alive, her V-8 heart
    catching Cerberus's ear.
But it was too late for him—our badness had started
    and now it rolled onto the street, the motor gassed, revved.
It was beautiful—the reckless, dizzy, happy motion exercised
    by my rods, exemplified by Sharon on my lap,
Sharon who would sit on the lap of anybody that was skipping school
    or had a car, and God I was doing both!
Tim and Carla were in the back, his tongue already down
    her throat, the wind filling the car,
Sharon's hair filling my face, her hand on my crotch,
    the curve in my pants, the curve in the road,

it was all so right, so perfectly wrong—
       then the swing of the car, the slow swift arc
of the world, Tim biting Carla's tongue, the spin
       waking him from his dizzy lust,
my Fury backwards, the pipe music created
       when rubber and pavement feel each other out
to a stop.
       When we got back to school,
there was hairless Cerberus, ushering us back to hell,
       our Fury tested, the curves in us
that needed to be swung swung, the four of us bad
       for good.

Romance, Exactly as I Remember It,

is how
the moon rises
full
every night
and the line it marches
is always taut
with hopes of young lovers
tonguing their troubles
into a place their mouths
can hardly contain.
The rising moon knows
every kiss
ever made between fire escape bars,
it knows every Johnny Mathis tune,
it knows absolutely
nothing else.
It empties itself
every 28 days,
and that is why
young lovers
feel new
as the tide pulls up
onto their feet
like a blanket
they will never toss off.

In their mouths,
    in the moon's mouth,
        promises are discovered
  amid salt and sugar,
    and all these white things
    swell into a larger kiss
      that will eclipse
only in the shadow
  of their own smart,
    slowly travelling
     bodies.

          (after Edwin Romond)

Guilt

It sneaks up on you,
maybe lies in your bed.
It whispers three good reasons you are a bastard:
    for all you've stolen,
    for all you've done to her,
    and for pissing on Mrs. Johnson's cat last night.
You ask if there's some mistake—
    it moans at the stupidity of your asking.
You ask to remedy your bastardhood.
It is then that it stands upright,
                200 feet tall,
looks down,
                sticks its giant toenail
    through the one part of your body
            you've always held as sacred,
and bolts the shrinking door shut.

It is now just you and your guilt,
    stuck in this space,
no card games,
            nobody talking,
staring at each other,
    waiting for the answers
that neither has the power to give.

Coming Clean

The phone rings. A woman tells me I'm doomed,
she has a voodoo doll of me,

and hangs up. Immediately I know it's true—
I've been having pains for weeks.

My wife would have nothing to do
with these aches, and referred me to my mother,

who insisted on having everything to do with them.
So I went to the doctor, who put my pain

under lights, opened it, listened to it,
descended into it with all his technology

and found nothing. This is how it deepened.
Whatever it was, I knew it wasn't something

to be found in the local, the body.
When the call came long distance with my answer,

I was actually grateful. Now I turn
to the windowsill, to the pile of chain letters

from Latvia I've been receiving, the ones
I haven't been mailing forth, and know

this is all connected, how the tide of black magic
can cross any ocean. I am a sinner

and turn back the clock of my heart
to recount all my heart-felt sins—

the ones that, if there is a hell,
and if it isn't like this, might itch a little

for punishment. The time I felt my friend Karen's ass,
wanting her more than any car, even at 17.

I apologized later, but we know how those things go.
The only thing I regretted was that she didn't like it.

So I apologize now. And to Mr. Romond,
11th grade English teacher who promised us all

Look Homeward, Angel would get better.
I'm sorry, Mr. Romond, for I have sinned.

All eight hundred pages of your book,
which I said I lost, are ashes

somewhere in an old campfire pit.
That night, literature made me feel so warm.

And the great poet, Stephen Dunn—I won't tell you
what I've done—just know it was horrible,

and you never realized it anyway.
These are all petty larcenies of the heart—

small pleasures I've stolen and can't give back,
or wouldn't. The letters accumulate and the pains

I take to right my life grow sharper.
In the distance, BJ Ward is a doll

and that image is tearing me apart.

The Classics in Couplets

(Written after overhearing a student complain,
"Cliff Notes are too long.")

The Odyssey
He got lost.
He paid the cost.

Hamlet
Uncle married mother.
    Oh brother....

Waiting for Godot
I don't hear him comin'—
Boy, am I bummin'.

The Love Song of J. Alfred Prufrock
No calls for a week.
Am I a geek?

Oedipus Rex
Oh brother—
I married mother!

Afraid of My Own Snoring

(for George Cruys)

20 too far behind and 30
around the corner, I went into the woods
alone. The fire was small but sufficient
enough to warm but not hurt me.

The burnt-edged hot dog was good, better
because of hunger, and the clouds held promise
enough for me to pitch my tent. If wind
blew strong, I would have to lie and let her

do what damage was in her invisible, fluid,
long bones. The tent flapped its skins
for hours, and the whole world
about me became alive—too alive. Wood

became less hard, softened with my own startled blood.
And, as I started to sleep, an enormous bear
came to my tent, moaned a low hungry tone,
enough to stir me from the gourmet, home-cooked food

I was lying with in my dreams.
I checked outside, swung my flashlight
all around, saw nothing but woods
that now seemed still. Even the breeze

had stopped. Settling back to sleep,
the bear came again, this time closer
than he sounded before, with his low threatening
groan. I jumped from my sleep, not as deep

as the darkness around me, and again
spread my light, my only weapon against the dark
and the things the dark held. Again, nothing
came of it. It happened twice more, the sleep and the din

of the bear's throat, and still there was nothing in it.
I did not sleep anymore after that—just lay
waiting for the bear's return. He never came,
I never slept, and wasted the meat of the night.

As I left the woods at dawn, it occurred
to me how that bear came only when it knew,
somehow, my eyes were elsewhere, somewhere
inward, and that is when he could be heard.

The bear, the woods, everything threatening was still—
I should have slept more soundly through my fears
in the trees—looked inward, and stayed there, instead
of being shook and ruled by such an invisible thrill.

A Quiet Day in Newark

Finally—finally I can hear the birds.
They chirp slowly. They sound like chimes made of sugar.
All the cars have stopped.
People are standing in doorways,
motionless. I hear the birds—they are beautiful.
A block away there is a woman crying. All this
is all I hear. She cries as if her mouth were the only door
to let pain out her body. The grammar school across the street
never makes noise—it has no windows to let in light
or bullets. A young man sticks his head out
a tenement window, slowly—a bead of sweat runs from his shiny head
onto the uneven sidewalk below. One woman's shoe lies unperturbed
on Clinton. Another person, this one also a woman,
moves silently from a candy shop. Her eyes move quickly,
side to side—two startled animals. A car starts crawling up Clinton
again, and I still peer from behind my dashboard.
There is headshaking now, nervous laughter
from men who almost live in hardware stores. Yes, now the world
seems to be rotating again—there is movement
in cars, on foot, in baby carriages.
I sit up straight, just as I was
before the four teens came running down the alley,
swinging guns like banners for freedom
in a war I've not fought. I shift
into drive, let my foot off the brake,
move slowly up Clinton, just as I was
before these four children brought life
into this dead city, blasting noise out, ricocheting

into pavement and flesh, moving all bystanders inside
themselves, tucked under cars, arches, the wings
we have grown and carry not to fly with
but to keep ourselves hidden.

Instant Sundance

(Lakota Sioux Rosebud Reservation, July 24–27, 1992)
for Tim Provencal

Take a tree—a great tree—
    hang parts of your life from it.
Friends will help.

Move your feet a little—
    a little in all directions.
As you travel outward, travel inward.

Before, during, and after,
    you must sweat.
Pour out all your poisons and promises

and love the human nation.
    Once you are dry
of hubris, of fear of disappointment,

once you have washed yourself
    with the rocks and water
you dredge up from inside,

you must become equally hard and soft
    until "balance" is the dance
you do with the tree in the changing wind.

You must know when to lift—
　　let your body fill the sky as birds do—
know when to place, each footstep

a bucket of soul emptying into the earth
　　as the sky fills the tree.
Thank the circle you're in—

thank the ground for its wide embrace,
　　thank the sisters and brothers around you,
holding flowers like important messages,

and thank your own body, a temple today—
　　the hands for clearing the land,
the torso for moving in holy sentences,

the hair for flying like your spirit,
　　your breath for massaging the chapel,
and your throat, your waterless throat,

for carrying the wind to your lungs,
　　for carrying your scream to Grandfather,
and for the scream itself, punctuating

like part of a lost heartbeat
　　that all doctors had given up on,
now suddenly glowing in the medicine of the breeze.

Letter to Some Students Whom I May Never
See Again after a Five-Day Writing Workshop

When you suffer, I hope you suffer miserably.
Is that what is appropriate here?
When you love, I hope you love without hope.
When happy, I hope you are blind
    only some of the time.
                      I hope your emotions
become the ocean
        you have only half-charted;
let them bathe you with their unknown waters,
and let those waters run as deep and long
    as you can possibly bear.

                You want advice?
Let your pen be a life-line,

    let it bleed
          where you have been most cut,
or use it when you need to cut yourself.

Is my metaphor too grand? Perhaps your pen
    should never be more than pen. Perhaps you
should always realize that. Perhaps your pen
    should be what you never leave—
          let your words live without you.

Be the mother who has lost the child
to the world it must now be a part of.
Be the father who never knew the child anyway.
    Stand on the shores of your poems and wave goodbye
as the waters carry that craft to the end of its world,
    where surely it will plunge into nothing.

And if there is dirt,
                                if the craft strikes land,
    may the discovery of that New World
            be a constant surprise
                        that carries you inland,

and as you discover the pools inside you
                may you explore them with the same thirst.

To be human is to let go the hand of God,
    and so you, the creator, have to let your work be human:
            let the reader have your words,
                    let emotion examine its own name.
    Let the hope of nothing,   of an end,
                be where you begin.
    When letting go,

                        say goodbye with both hands.

Dancing with the Teacher

(for Maureen Kosa)

What a fiery teacher she was!
    Not knowing any better,
I engaged her

in verbal banter—she loved Huck Finn
    and I loved Huck Finn
and the whole class,

the whole world could go to hell
    for all I cared.
She took the first step and I took

her hand and soon we were rocking on that raft
    with Huck and Jim, doing the rumba,
the jitterbug, the twist—

we got down and let out—
    we didn't stop
with the whole class gawking,

amazed that literature could shake us,
    that mere words
could create such dizzy abandon,

could move us so violently,
        our bodies twenty years apart
but so close together, in sync.

When Shakespeare entered the room
        we turned the lights low,
pulled down the shades,

did a slow waltz, timing our dips
        with Hamlet's,
our shifts with Petruchio's.

But when Whitman came along,
        forget it!
Open the windows! Throw on the lights!

We hucklebucked, hully gullied, shook, shimmied,
        and locomotioned! We swung our bodies
and never let down!

The class was amazed—
        some caught on quick,
took that heat in,

and soon everyone broke loose—
        the charleston! the boogaloo! the handjive!
Mrs. Kosa madisoned, Jen Faber mashed potatoed,

Jake and Brett tangoed—even Jerome Higgins stood up
        and did the watusi!
Everyone was dancing

with the freedom hips were born with,
        the freedom of knees,
arms, torsos, necks—

the freedom to read
        in other people's moves
a wildness greater than our own,

and the freedom to pick up,
        to learn how to be that wild
with our own steps in time.

Learning German

In German class they tell me about stressed places,
how my diction is too soft—that the language
can only be spoken with hard and soft.
There's half a globe making hard sounds,
saying the same things the other half does
with softer sounds—our thoughts are the same.

       •   •

A girl with a hard tongue kissed me once.
It was new, different—she seemed old in my mouth.
It was outside, in her backyard—
there was no moon, no stars—I wallowed
between her rigidness and the cool hug
of the earth. When it was over,
there was some of my softness
in her, some of her hardness in me.

       •   •

If I whisper
             marrow, pelt, horn
would you understand
somehow?

       •   •

I know parents who start loving softly
and realize how hard it is.

                              It
starts the same—a look, a word,
a fist—they are soon full of fists.
They say Love is hard. I say love
was never meant to be all-soft or all-hard—

There is paper in oaks,
and oaks in paper.
It is the moment we look at it
that matters—what form we catch it in.

                    •   •

We differ only in softnesses,
        and where they are,
and how these places
        are affected by hardness.

                    •   •

I know men who are moments,
who tried to love hard and found
how soft it is.
                    You know
them too—maybe in some bar,
maybe your lunchroom, maybe
you've been loved by one
or raised someone who was.

They're the men who sit in corners
and smell whiskey-thick—they're
the assured moments of a place you frequent,
the moments you try to avoid.
They crouch and mutter to themselves,
turning and watching their hands
whose palms wear the slow blankets of calluses.

       •   •

We differ only in hardnesses,
    and where they are,
and how these places
    are affected by softness.

       •   •

Have you ever lived your life hard/soft?
Perhaps in your work, or your love?
The way your hand touches, responds, touches—
the way your tongue moves when you speak.
Have you ever learned to say "fuck"
to your lover? Surely you know the balance
of hard and soft, where they touch,
and how they bend to meet.

       •   •

And my tongue wants to bend like that,
Wants to have both marrow and horn, palms
and knuckles, wood and pulp—
it wants to border them,
ride out the space between them,
and moisten everything it touches.
This is how I will learn German;
how, like any language,
it must be spoken with everything I have.

•

The Appendix Poem

Have you taken out what won't work?
Have you prodded it,
        made sure it was deathly sick?
    Did you wash your hands first?

Have you severed and dissected, seen its dirt?

      You still don't know, do you?
   Its secret is an explosion,
        not a nick.

And I've seen explosions better than you.

I've seen poems,
     so tell me,

         did it burst?

Acknowledgments

Gratitude and acknowledgment to the editors of the publications in whose pages the following poems (or earlier versions of them) in *Jackleg Opera: New Poems* first appeared:

5 AM: The Closer

The American Poetry Review: Ode to the Middle Finger

Controlled Burn: Hee Blow; No Job, No Money, No Girlfriend; Shotgun Wedding 2006

Edison Literary Review: When I Submitted "Stopping by Woods on a Snowy Evening" to My Workshop; Upon Reading *Plato's Allegory of the Cave* on a Smart Phone

Green Mountains Review: Baseball 1980

Imagination & Place: To the Turtle

Inside Jersey: Development; The Photographer's Divorce

Journal of New Jersey Poets: Building Codes; Compassion

The Literary Review: 17 Becomes 43

Nightsun: Disgusted with the Endless War, I Turn Off the Evening News and Make Love to My Wife Instead

The Normal School: Resurrection

Painted Bride Quarterly: Bruce Springsteen and Jimmy Vivino Jam at Convention Hall, Asbury Park

The Paulinskill Poetry Project: Voices from Here: Book Tour: Another Barnes & Noble—Empty Chairs and Good Coffee

Poetry: Cuckoldom

RATTLE: Wolverine the X-Man Kisses

The Rutherford Red Wheelbarrow: A Late Memoriam for Tommy Whuzizname, Because Nobody Ever Talks about That Prick Anymore

Stillwater Review: Jack & Jill; To the Pussycat

Tiferet: At the Party: "So What Do You Do?"

U.S. 1 Worksheets: Ars Poetica; Babyproofing; Naming the Growth; Portrait of the Artist as Egg Salad

Also, "The Star-Ledger" (in *Gravedigger's Birthday*) first appeared in *Poetry*.

Thank you to the New Jersey State Council on the Arts for
a Distinguished Artist Fellowship that proved essential for the
composition of this book. Thanks also to the Virginia Center for the
Creative Arts for the space and time to develop many of these poems,
and much gratitude to the Geraldine R. Dodge Foundation for grants
that enabled my residencies there.

Thank you to the following people whose generosity of spirit (among
other things) has helped in the composition of these poems:

My mother, father, and brother—how my love for you further
deepens with age. Ben Lapinski, true sensei. Brian Bradford, the
Paragon of Human Evolution. Kevin Lopatin and Eric Johnson, the
long-haul truckers I share this road with. Thanks to Ginger for what
we had and what we have. Charles Rafferty—my friend and my only
close reader for all four of these books. Nick Ingram—who loves to
root for the Phils and feels love down to her roots—you're my sister.
That Roaring Thundergust, George Cruys, Devourer of Mountains.
Doc Tatu, who helped me out of a hole and held it all together for me.
Laurie Granieri, the light I followed home. Sandy Zulauf, co-founder
of the W.C. Fields Academy of Higher Living. The plainclothes friar
and confidant, Joseph G. Skudera Jr. The gracious Gayle and Harry
Carrick—who put their property (and low insurance rates) in danger
by inviting me into their house every February. Beth Anne Vogel—
Pablo didn't thank you in his book, so I thank you here. As always,
gratitude to all my teachers—especially Stephen Dunn, my guide in
things both ethereal and carnal. And, of course, to Richard Grossinger,
Lindy Hough, Doug Reil, my project editor Jessica Sevey, copy editor
Adrienne Armstrong, cover designer Jasmine Hromjak, and everyone
else at North Atlantic Books. Your support over the past twenty years
has been munificent and thoroughly appreciated.

Thanks especially to Dylan, my son, for reminding me that there are
answers for seemingly unanswered questions.

About the Author

BJ Ward's poems have been published in *Poetry, The American Poetry Review, TriQuarterly, Painted Bride Quarterly, The New York Times,* and other publications. He is the recipient of a Pushcart Prize and two Distinguished Artist Fellowships from the NJ State Council on the Arts. He teaches in the Creative Writing program at Warren County Community College in New Jersey.

The Io Poetry Series

The Io Poetry Series honors the career work of poets who express the depth, breadth, and scope of subject matter of *Io* and North Atlantic Books. The Series pays tribute to North Atlantic Books' literary roots in *Io*, the interdisciplinary journal founded by Lindy Hough, Richard Grossinger, and colleagues in 1964. *Io*'s single-subject issues laid the groundwork for North Atlantic Books' literary publishing of subsequent decades. The poets in this series either appeared in the journal, were working concurrently, or preceded and inspired *Io*.

Westport Poems
Jonathan Towers

Heavenly Tree,
Northern Earth
Gerrit Lansing

The Intent On:
Collected Poems, 1962–2006
Kenneth Irby

Wild Horses, Wild Dreams:
New and Selected Poems,
1971–2010
Lindy Hough

Collected Poems
of Lenore Kandel
Lenore Kandel

Catching Light:
Collected Poems
of Joanna McClure
Joanna McClure